Sunday Adelaja

HOW TO OVERCOME THE FEAR OF DEATH

Sunday Adelaja

HOW TO OVERCOME THE FEAR OF DEATH
©2017

ISBN 978-617-7394-00-5

It is not just an assumption that this book could help you overcome the fear of death, it is indeed a reality. I had written this book originally in Russian language, after which many people that were so afraid of death started coming to me rejoicing about the prospect of dying. Having read the book they could get a clear picture of what death is and what to expect in death, thereby overcoming the fear of death which is hidden in the unknown.

Cover Design by Olexandr Bondaruk

HOW TO OVERCOME THE FEAR OF DEATH
Golden Pen Limited,
Milton Keynes, United Kingdom

Contents

PREFACE

Death is a menace. Most of not all of mankind are afraid of it. Is it really possible not to be afraid of death? This book is aimed at helping humanity overcome the fear of death.

Year in, year out polls and surveys constantly show that the fear of death is the most prevalent form of fear that plagues mankind. In this book, I have endeavoured to paint the picture of the bliss and excitement of death. A major reason why people fear death is because of what they don't know. Most people don't know what to expect after death which explains the reason for the fear. Humans will normally fear the unknown. My approach in this book is to expose us to what happens to a person immediately after he dies and the times afterwards.

It is not just an assumption that this book could help you overcome the fear of death, it is indeed a reality. I had written this book originally in Russian language, after which many people that were so afraid of death started coming to me rejoicing about the prospect of dying. Having read the book they could get a clear picture of what death is and what to expect in death, thereby overcoming the fear of death which is hidden in the unknown.

This is only one point out of many in this book. By the time you finish exploring this book, it could probably become your favourite book after the bible. For I know of many people who now sleep with this book by their bed side. Such is the assurance they gained of the afterlife.

As I was compiling the list of 50 books to release on my 50th birthday anniversary, I felt it necessary to include this particular topic - how to overcome the fear of death. The victory over this particular fear will affect your life on earth more so, it will affect your relationship with the lord. You will see a change and a difference in your attitude to others. Get ready for an exciting journey as you read this book. Godspeed.

For the Love of God, Church and Nation

Dr. Sunday Adelaja.

INTRODUCTION

At the dawn of the twentieth century, God gave Seneca Sodi who was in a coma, the priceless experience of spending forty days in Heaven. Here's how it happened.

I had momentary thoughts flung across my mind: "Is this really death? Am I really going to say goodbye to worldly things today? Am I truly in the borderland of eternity? If so, blessed victory!"

The next thing I observed was that I was standing in one corner of the room looking with deep interest upon my body, which was lying in quiet repose upon the bed. I cannot describe enough the strange, yet joyful feeling of my soul on finding myself released from the body. I walked forward and stood beside the bed and with mingled feelings of joy and pity, I said to my body, "I feel sorry to leave you behind, but you are still mortal and will be till the resurrection". I found that my vision was greatly improved since being freed from the mortal body - nor did I regret, now I was released, for everything seemed to shine with a luster and glow, with a brightness I had never known before; and what seemed more remarkable still, was that the sunlight did not aid me in any sense to comprehend things about me, for I knew that at night when all the world were asleep and that it was entirely dark to outward human eyes, yet to me everything shone with splendor grander than the brightest noonday the Earth ever afforded.

I next saw three angels with me who seemed busy with some peculiar embalming process for my body, which I did not understand. They spoke to me most pleasantly and said: "Be not afraid. We have come as your escorts for your Heavenly home, the light of which shines so brightly upon you now."

The angels now began to sing, and oh, such sweet music I've never heard while in the body. When they had finished the anthem, they said, "Will you now follow us?" When we had stepped outside, I saw the chariot which seemed to be made of light. It was standing still at the threshold. I tried to say goodbye to my sleeping body, my old home, and my two servants when the angels hastened me to a seat with them in a chariot. They again assured me of a safe journey homeward. In a moment more the chariot began to rise with a swift and noiseless motion and to me with an unknown speed, we were going on our flight toward the eternal mansions. No sooner had I taken my seat in the chariot then I found I could converse with the angels with perfect freedom. There seemed to be a kind of comprehension of ideas without the effort of words. I looked out of the chariot again and saw we were passing with indescribable speed. The Earth with its cities, towns, and mountains were vanishing like a specter in the distance. We soon seemed to have the moon under our feet as we mounted the pillars of the Heavens. We had many conversations on the way. I found the angels most tender and lovely beings, so full of instructions and helpfulness; my soul loved them exceedingly. I felt as though I was acquainted with the Heavenly kingdom, for the angels had

told me so much. As I would look abroad from the chariot window, the stars could be seen everywhere just as I had always seen them from Earth; I knew then we had not gone beyond the regions of the solar system, so I asked the angel:

"Where is Heaven?"

"Oh", said he, "it is not far away. The Earth is the first habitation of man, and while he is of the Earth he is Earthly in his nature. Heaven is the future and everlasting habitation of all those who have prepared themselves for it. You will soon find that my words are true that Heaven is not far away. Your Father's love and care have provided both these worlds for you. Your Heavenly home is your real home. The Earth was only your birthplace, the place of your beginning. When God gave you eternal life He connected you with all Heavenly realms, for He gave you His life which has always been. Look and see..." (1)

Dear reader, I hope you realize that the book you hold in your hand is a journey into life's true home; Heaven. We will explore stories of people who have managed to see a part of life in Heaven, to also have a glimpse of the future life after our physical death. And, if today you're afraid to die, it comes from not knowing what awaits you after your journey here on Earth. To overcome the fear of death, we must examine the experience of those who know what kind of life awaits us in Heaven, and the benefits, and throughout their Earthly existence strived to become heirs of Heaven.

What are the emotions we often witness when there is a funeral procession? As a rule, they are grief and mourning for the dead person. However, what if we knew that death brings the possibility for acquiring a true life. You probably would not grief, but will joyfully and cheerfully say goodbye to those who gained something more than just life on Earth.

What do you know about Heaven except that it's the space above the Earth? This is probably all that most people on our planet know about Heaven. However, not knowing the true purpose of Heaven limits our concept of death with a single feeling – fear. The fear of death is usually the most prominent in life this is because uncertainty is always frightening. Imagine you find yourself in an unknown room, you cannot see anything around, and it's so dark that movement is limited. You have no idea where you are and what is happening around you. Under such circumstances, your imagination is hardly going to provide a positive picture in your head, and the mood will certainly not be good, it will be one of restlessness, and most likely, you'll be racked with fear. It will be hard to cope with your thoughts in that place. But, as soon as the light is turned on and you see the room, its layout and the environment, the fear will certainly let go. Why does this happen? It's simple: you see what's around you, and know what to expect. You have the idea of what is going on and you are no longer scared.

If only people knew what death is! If they knew what opportunities await them in Heaven, Death would be an

acquisition, and death would be seen as the chance for a new and a full life in Heaven.

With the help of this book dear friends, we are going to shed light on such a great reward in the life of every human being, the acquisition of Heaven. We'll get all the necessary knowledge that will dispel the fear of death, and we will grasp how to live our lives here on Earth, anticipating joyfully the end of our stay, and the eagerly awaiting a great heritage of life in Heaven.

Heaven... Heaven... Heaven... It is not just the space above the Earth, It is a beautiful place of abode which begins a real life for us. One with millions of exciting feelings and opportunities that are concealed from us, here on Earth. All these are concealed up to a certain time and that time is till the moment of our death.

Dear friends, let's begin an exhilarating flight to Heaven! Turn on your imagination as we need to see Heaven, we will then start to live for Heaven while we are here on Earth, so that every day of this life helps us achieve this result.

We cannot be selfish and unloving in one life, and generous and loving in the next; the two lives are too closely blended – one but a continuation of the other.

Frank Springer
(From Within Heaven's Gates by Rebecca Rutter Springer)

PRACTICAL RECOMMENDATIONS ON READING THIS BOOK

THIS BOOK CAN CHANGE YOUR LIFE!

Dear reader, you hold a book whose title is of interest and relevant to you.

Often under the influence of what we read, we make a decision to change our way of life, but after a while, we forget our intentions, allowing mundane things and vanity to overtake us. So, the book you are holding in your hand is not another accumulation of knowledge. It is a book with the potential of changing your life. Therefore, to be transformed by this book, I suggest some practical recommendations.

1. Read this book several times

Don't be in a rush, read thoughtfully. Ask yourself how and when you will be able to apply the information you acquired. Carefully study the book, analyzing yourself afterwards.

2. Read aloud

Reading aloud allows us to release that force which stands behind each word in our life. It helps us not only to see each word but also to hear it. Spoken words have a waved nature and when sound is released, it has a transforming impact on all surrounding objects and subjects. Thus, words matter. Don't neglect the power of words! Don't let the power in words which is capable of changing your life and circumstances pass you by!

3. Underline and add notes

While reading this book, keep a pen or a highlighter (felt-tip pen) ready. Underline separate lines of the text and paragraphs, this simple action will triple your ability to memorize. On fields of this book, write down your own thoughts and make notes. Let this book become YOUR book. Underlining helps the process of reading, makes it more interesting and helps us to look through the book again.

4. Reread underlined fragments

Underlining and marking will help you skim through the most important questions and fragments of this book again. Also, to be able to digest the reading, you will need to get back to it as often as possible.

Let the highlighted fragments inspire you to make your life better. We possess an amazing ability to forget. The only way to memorize the necessary information for you is to come back to it over and over again.

5. Immediately apply the learned principles

A person can't be taught anything, he can only learn. It means that training is an active process. Best of all, we learn with practice. If you wish to seize the principles provided in this book, use them as often as possible and at any given opportunity. If you don't practice them, you will forget everything very quickly. Only what is put to practice, remains in your memory.

6. Give priority to what you learn

At the end of each chapter, you will find the Golden truth, which accumulates all important thoughts throughout the chapter. There are tests that will help you to assess yourself and your skill, and practical tasks that will help you bring what you read to life. They are not just to read, but to help you get the maximum results and benefits of practical exercises, I suggest that you execute them within 24 hours, otherwise covered by the bustle of life, you will again alienate your destiny, and those changes you are expecting in your life will not happen.

Due to many years of experience collaborating with people, I have realized that they usually perform similar tasks «just for the show». But, you are not in school, where you can get away with all sorts of excuses. It is your life that is at stake, and the fulfillment of these tasks will define how it will change you. Therefore, I ask you to take these tasks seriously because it is vital; not for the author, but for you. It is preferable to find a quiet place where nobody can disturb you, in order to work with the tasks. Perhaps

there will be a time when no one is at home or a night time when everyone is asleep and no one can disturb you.

Be sure to reflect on the previous chapter, on all the points that you have highlighted, think of your decisions and record all subsequent actions. Do not forget to schedule specific time periods to determine the limitations encountered. This will help you not to postpone the plan for the life changing steps. Find someone to whom you report to regarding your decisions and who might remind you or be a partner to work on your self-improvement.

Record the date when you start reading this book

_____

Let this date be the turning point in your life!

RECOMMENDATIONS ON THE IMPLEMENTATION OF PRACTICAL TASKS

1. After reading each chapter, reflect on each point; think back to what caught your attention, the most or the things you noted for yourself. Remember your thoughts and write all subsequent actions.

2. Decisions should be made immediately; and you have 24 hours to put any of them into action.

3. Set the terms and limitations for yourself, it helps you focus on the realization of your decisions.

Chapter 1

THE ADVANTAGE
OF DEATH

Chapter 1
THE ADVANTAGE
OF DEATH

Can death be sleep, when life is but a dream, And scenes of bliss pass as a phantom by? The transient pleasures as a vision seem, And yet we think the greatest pain's to die.

- John Keats

D espite the fact the lines of this poem can be rather difficult to grasp, death is inevitable for every living person on Earth. Death is stronger than life, and there is still no one who would not die. Death is stronger than beauty, because beauty is a temporary state, regardless of whether a person is rich or poor, lives in the US or China, death is inevitable for everyone. Therefore, this book is written in order to provide an appropriate knowledge about Eternity. After all, each of us will have to die. Therefore, it is important to prepare. For after death, we could enjoy the true understanding of life and its exciting beginning in Heaven.

ARE YOU READY TO DIE TODAY OR TOMORROW?

«Why did this happen to our family? How could this happen? Why so early? I'm not ready to let you go! ...

These words were a cry of the soul for a young girl who could not accept the premature death of her brother.

He was 27 years old. Life had just begun, he had so much ahead of him ... And, death has just put an end to all his dreams and aspirations. Was there someone in the family prepared for it to happen so early? Was anyone prepared for this? No! However, it is impossible to escape from death. This is what happened in this family.

Helga, this was the name of the girl who could not recover from such terrible and unexpected loss. She was not afraid of death. She was worried about only one question: what's next? It was not scary to say goodbye to a dead body or to listen to the words of sympathy from others. She was interested in one thing: whether she will be able to meet such a person, who was not only a relative, but a real brother, friend, father, and a really close person. The person, who always defended, forgave, and taught his sister, the one who loved her no matter what. He was just there, always, even when she did not ask about it. Therefore, it was a priority for young Helga to live in accordance with such a short Earthly life of her brother to forgive and to love, to hurry to live today, and not to wait for tomorrow.

Because, in fact, tomorrow may never come.

In this family, as well as in any other, no one was prepared for the death of a loved one. Nobody wants that to happen either today or tomorrow or ever in the future. Many people say that death does not exist, but listen, it is inevitable. According to global statistics, which tracks the dynamics of the population of the Earth in real time, at least one person dies every second in the world. According to a data listed on the site, more than 150 thousand people die within one day. **Hence, when some people are born, others are dying at the same time.** Furthermore, whether we will be just part of the statistics or will leave some significant trace, will determine where we spend eternity, in Heaven or in Hell. There is a huge chance to become a part of a great eternity if we will live for Heaven, and not just for the satisfaction of our own desires.

So, what is your own attitude toward death? Are you ready to die today or tomorrow? You can argue that this is not a kind of question that you need to know the answer. Besides, you're still young, and this is the issue of the final period of life. However, as it is shown in the previous story of the death of a young boy, death cannot be determined by age. None of us knows the day of our death. However, if we knew that death is actually our acquisition, we would remove the fear of death from our lives. Let us try to gain an understanding about everything in order to look the «enemy» in the face.

I have come to regard death like an old debt, at long last to be discharged.

- Albert Einstein,
(Theoretical Physicist, public figure and humanist)

According to Albert Einstein, despite our wishes, we will have to pay our debts. In this case, if we will refuse to pay, this would be done by force. Dear friend, in order to be prepared for what will happen after death; we have to live today as if tomorrow we could die. But, do not think that you can live the way you like. No, you should live a worthful life. It is not necessary to wait for old age, sickness, infirmity, to reflect on the quality of life and its consequences. We must «die» today and every day to our personal desires and do everything possible, in order to taste the beauty of life in Heaven.

Live in Heaven is:

To live and act according to our conscience and not to deceive anyone.

Not to focus only on our own interests and concerns, while not seeing people around us or their problems.

To do good things, as much as possible, no matter who needs it - a close person, or the stranger.

To live in love. To love God, people, life itself - in short, everything that surrounds you.

To try to seek a meeting with the one who gave you life - Your Creator.

Regardless of your beliefs, God is the one who gave you life, You were not just born because your parents came together. **Your life has been given to you by the Creator, and you just rented it for a certain period of time.** Many parents planned to have a child, though not all made this plan to bring a life to earth. Therefore, we assume that the birth of a child is the decision of two people. However, «Man proposes but God disposes,» so the decision about creating a new life, actually, does not depend on us.

If today we have this life, whether we have to think about what awaits us at the end of life and what will happen after we die? Will it be the acquisition, and whether we have to spend so much time and internal resources on the fear of death, clutching for life as the only chance? Hence, if you do not know the answers to these questions, we are going to acquire all the necessary knowledge from this book. However, in order to have an idea of what life can be in Heaven, we have to imagine how it looks. What is Heaven and what prospects does it open up for its «guests»? Therefore, with the help of a wide range of stories, we will paint the canvas of life after death.

In case you are afraid of death then start living for eternity, and not for the sake of temporary pleasure, and the fear of death will disappear once and for all because you will be living in anticipation of Heaven. When we experience hunger, the refrigerator becomes a magnet for us. However, imagine that for example, you have a desire to eat ice cream at this very moment, you feel the taste of this delicacy with all the particle of your body. I'm sure you've read such books on how the body is transferred from one place to another with the help of thoughts. This suggests the phenomenal ability of our mind, which we will be able to use when we will be living in Heaven.

Is it actually possible to presume that it will be boring in Heaven? In fact, our Earthly life is limited by a number of internal and external factors. But, in Heaven there is no money or the lust to be rich; there is only one thing; love. Boredom is an earthly concept, and we limit ourselves with it because we do not want to go beyond what is permitted, and beyond our comfort zone to stiffen and begin to live fully. If you find that loud laughter is bad, then you should know that you have limited your life with boredom and regulations that are not interesting to anyone. As for me, I appreciate every moment and try to live every moment while trying to leave boredom behind. I laugh all the time, while I hear others speak about my laughter and how it it heals them.

It cannot be boring in Heaven because all the senses will work synchronously there. For example, it is

a pleasure for everyone to hear the words of love. In Heaven, you will feel the pleasure of these words with every piece of your body. Everything will work only in one direction towards the feeling of joy and happiness. And, this joy will not be caused by any emotional outburst, or the fact that expectations were met as it is on earth. The feeling of happiness will be constant in Heaven and you will experience it always, and everything around you will radiate it. For example, you walk down the street and you are infinitely happy due to the road itself and the grass growing around. There is no need to get happiness from someone, as it is apart of your thoughts, words, and actions.

In real life, some relationships are excellent, while others may cause a feeling of hostility. Both scenario might benefit a certain people. But however,, the process of building relationships is given to us only to show what it means to love people with whom we communicate, to discover new emotions generated by these relationships. But in Heaven, there is no rejection or jealousy, and there is no need to defend your opinion because the love there is above all things. Everything is based only on mutual adoption and love for each other.

It cannot be boring when perfection is present. People spend their time bored and monotonous, thinking that life is wonderful, but then the fear of losing someone or something denies them the privilege of living fully. . During life, we are limited by financial resources, the scope of our

mind, and we do not allow ourselves to be happy. We are looking for the opportunity to enjoy anyone or anything in our lives. But in Heaven, everything will please us; even an ordinary tree will evoke a sense of joy and love, bringing us happiness.

Well, is it boring? Is it really boring to experience feelings in its entirety, when there is no need to hurry, worry about why something did not work? It cannot be boring when there is always a result, a range of positive emotions, where the eyes perceive the beauty, the ears hear the surf of happiness, where every touch is infinite tenderness. Therefore, by drawing such pictures of Heaven, I want to lift the curtain of our everyday look on it. You will see something that you should strive for, every day, bringing the picture of Heaven in your life.

Summary. Knowing where we are going and that time is slipping away quickly, we need to understand what awaits us at the finish line of life.

Mary K. Baxter shared the impressions of her journey to Heaven, the Kingdom of The Almighty God. Jesus gave her a vision of the future and gave her spiritual guidance:

«**The overwhelming beauty of what I saw around me was breathtaking!** The clothing the heavenly being wore looked like a brilliant garment of light. The angel had triangular-shaped wings that glistened with the colors of

the rainbow. Although, I was not surprised, I was amazed at the indescribable beauty that God made evident all around.»

That is the beauty that we could not see here on Earth, although we think that there is no place more beautiful. We are mistaken because we have not seen Heaven. Lots of lights, which you can watch and enjoy, and you do not want to blink and wipe your tears, because here, the eye cannot withstand the pressure of sunlight. Beauty is everywhere in Heaven, and it tells us that it is not necessary to go all over the world to see miracles because they are everywhere in Heaven.

"The magnificent gate that stood before me in splendor was made of a solid pearl."

In Heaven, everything is made in accordance with the highest standards. How about a gate or door of an apartment made of pearls, real pearls? This is at least impressive, and at best, extremely expensive. In Heaven, there is a lot of jewelry, which is why here, people in general and woman in particular, are so fond of jewelry because Heaven is the most precious place. This means that we must strive to live in Heaven.

«Suddenly, music filled the whole atmosphere. It was all around me. It was above me. It seemed to penetrate my very being. Wave after powerful wave of beautiful music, and singing, surged across the landscape and seemed to

envelop everything and everyone.

I could see diamonds-glittering, glistering, and exquisite diamonds, diamonds everywhere! Some were as large as blocks of concrete. Some of these diamonds seemed to be for the mansions of those who were soul winners on Earth. (3)

Heaven... How beautiful it is, so great and mighty. We see the wealth of the whole Earth, but have you seen somewhere with the gates of pearls? Have you seen the diamonds on the road, which would be just a kind of decoration? All that we admire here, what attracts us, the wealth and luxury, are already in Heaven and in abundance. In Heaven, beauty is everywhere, and there is no need to look for something that might surprise you, or bring you fun. You will admire everything around you because previously, we could not see all this in such superiority.

Heaven's light fills every cell of your body with warmth and comfort. Even the music is perceived not just by the human ears, it pervades the entire body as if it were in everything that is around.

Summary. *In order to get rid of the fear of death, it is crucial to see the beauty of Heaven, and it will be a bright motivation to live for others and not just for yourself.*

The information we will read in this book cannot be compared with everything that we have ever seen in our life. Knowing how beautiful life is in Heaven, each of us,

once and for all, would get rid of the fear of death and begin to live by thinking of it as an acquisition. After all, just imagine that everything surrounding you has a combination of the colors you want. Any rare delicacy you desire, you will savor with every cell of your body. Even the eyes, nails, skin, will get pleasure from what you see, say, or eat. You will be provided with a wide range of incredible meetings, conversations, and events, something that you cannot obtain while living here. Have you ever been in the United States, for example, in Antarctica? In Heaven, all this will be possible, according to the desires of your heart. Thus, there is no need to get a visa, obtain a permit and pay a lot of money. Do you want to swim in Niagara Falls? It is not a problem! Do you want to ski in the Alps? You are welcome! Or maybe you want to see an island of extraordinary beauty. All things are possible for those who dwell in Heaven.

There is still the fear of death? Begin to see all the possibilities of Heaven, and you will find out what will happen after your death. Live for Heaven every day.

Have you ever thought about what kind of life will emerge after death? Have you seen a funeral, the dead body, the cemetery and then think it's the end. If so, then, it is understandable why you have not won the fear of death. Because in death, you do not see the continuation of your life. Maybe you have a fascinating and interesting life here, but I will reveal a secret: it is just a pathetic copy of a real life in Heaven. Hence, our well-being in Heaven will depend

on the quality of each passing minute today.

Parable «*What happens after death*»

On that day, every visitor asked the teacher only one thing: what will happen after death? The teacher just smiled and said nothing. Then the disciples asked why he kept evading the answer.

- Have you ever noticed that the afterlife is interesting to people who do not know what to do in this life? They need another life that would last forever, said the teacher.

- Nevertheless, is there life after death or not? - Insisted one of his disciples.

- Is there life before death, that is the question, - said the teacher.

I just want to ask you, do you really live «until death»? Do you really live in such a manner so that you can confidently state: «Yes, I am ready to die today, and I have something to leave behind» Well, of course, except for the children. Are you living so that you can confidently say: «Yes, I am going to live in Heaven, and my place is there» But, only without the ideas, such as «Heaven and Hell is a fiction,» «I do not believe it», and so on. If you think so, then you simply have not studied this issue or simply are not faced with the risk of death face to face.

I have formed during the last few years such close relationships with this best and truest friend of mankind that death's image is not only no longer terrifying to me, but is indeed very soothing and consoling, and I thank my God for graciously granting me the opportunity...of learning that death is the key which unlocks the door to our true happiness.

Wolfgang Amadeus Mozart,
(An Austrian composer and virtuoso)

At the time of his death, Mozart was 34 years old, but he managed to leave a bright mark, despite the fact that he lived more than two hundred years ago. For him, based on his words, death was an acquisition and the main purpose of his existence. Mozart had raised an important point the «**opportunity to learn**» the meaning of life and death. This should be for us a hint that life and death, are the questions that each of us should study and not study from our own beliefs. Therefore, to understand and to respond to the question, what will life after death be like and whether it is boring in Heaven, we will try to study everything step by step.

SO, WHAT IS DEATH ACTUALLY?

The fear of death follows from the fact that people take very little from life, restricted by theirown false conception.

Leo Tolstoy
(Russian writer and thinker)

Our limited knowledge does not allow us to be ready for many things and events in our lives and especially for death. After all the subject of death is an abomination in many families as it is not accepted to talk about something that has a negative tone. Nobody will ever allow himself or herself to say that death is the acquisition, for only one reason; fear.

The fear of death limits our thoughts of it and does not allow us to live in freedom. How often do we hear: don't go there, don't do that thing, don't take risk, don't attempt doing more than you can imagine? Hence, we repeat the same phrase to our children as if their whole life is based on a self-preservation instinct, which brings about the question: what about the development and the success that can be achieved only by overcoming the difficulties? Candidly, it is going directly in such a way: seeing the obstacle, we stop, because of the self-preservation instinct. The fear of being deprived of life or to endure the pain that holds us bound, through the chains that we have created in our minds, not realizing that life does not end when we physically die.

From an early age, children were told that; «Life is good, but death .... I don't know what death is actually, but, undoubtedly, something bad. Bad enough not to be discussed or thought of. Hence, in the future, the theme of death will not be discussed at all. Well, you may not talk about it, but you know that it is going to happen sooner or later, which leads to another question; "If you know about some event and at the same time, do not prepare for it, what do you expect? Knowing the fact that death is inevitable, and the time of death is not dependent on age, so why not talk about this at least in order to prepare your family, and for yourself, to interpret it not as a loss, but rather as the acquisition of life. For example, I would be surprised to hear from the driver, who is going on a trip to an unknown place that he will drive the car undirected. Not having studied the route, without looking at the map on the destination or not having considered the route ahead, and just will sit in the car, saying, «I don't know how, but I will reach the place.» **Intuition is good, but the clear mind is much better.** Many of you will agree with this.

Summary. *In order to know the prospect of death, it is necessary to study this subject and to have the answer for the question, what will happen after your life's journey. And before this event it is important to know what your further life would look like.*

Then, it turns out that we know the path of our life and we know that it will end with death. Nevertheless, we do not prepare for this and even are not interested in our

future life, and where we will spend eternity in Heaven or in Hell. Answers to these questions would improve our quality of life at the finish line, and would release us from our fear of death. Everyone wants to live in paradise, but few people know that there are special conditions for life on Earth, which provide an eternity in Heaven. However, you will argue that it is indecent to talk about the thing that destroys the world in the heart to talk about death. Besides, it involves negative thoughts, and how to think about something that has not happened yet?

But, would it be «decent» to die and not start to live? Is it possible to think about death when you will be gone? Moreover, why not prepare for life in Heaven right now, you may not have time for this at all?

Man is the only animal who knows he will die and man alone questions death as an inevitable phenomenon.

Stephen William Hawking
(Theoretical physicist)

Yes, maybe it is rude to call man an animal. But if we live today only with our instincts and stimulus. To sleep, to eat and to go to work without having a personal interest, and not carry out any analysis, then, indeed, it begs comparison with animals. We know that we are not immortal, but few are preparing for death, or think about eternity. It is easier to live thinking that eventually, somehow, we will find out. But as a rule, we do not have the time.

JOKE

Doorbell. A guy opens, and there stands death in front of him. All in laces, bows and with balloons. A guy:
- Who are you?
- Death.
- But, why are you in laces and with balloons?
- Ridiculous.

All this would be funny if it was not so sad. When death comes, it does not ask whether we like it or not, it does not wait for an opportunity, it does not always come to the old or sick, sometimes it just happens, not asking for anything.

Death is the cessation of life. It is a stop of all biological and physiological processes of the body's vital functions.

According to the Andrei Gnezdilov, Professor of psychiatry St. Petersburg Medical Academy of Postgraduate Education and Scientific Director of the Gerontology Department:

Death is not the end and not the destruction of our personality. It is just a change of the state of our consciousness after the Earthly life. I worked in the oncology clinic for ten years, and now, for more than twenty years, I am working in hospice. During these years of dialogue with the seriously ill and dying people, I have had the opportunity to make sure that human consciousness does not disappear after death. I found out that our body is just a shell, which leaves the soul at the moment of transition to another world.

All this is proved by numerous stories of people who have been in such a state of «spiritual» consciousness during clinical death. When people tell me about some of their secrets, the wide experience of the medical practitioner allows me to confidently distinguish hallucinations from real events.

Neither I nor anyone else cannot explain these phenomena in terms of science. Science does not cover all the knowledge about the world. However, there are facts proving that in addition to our world there is another world that acts by unknown laws and is beyond our comprehension.

This world, in which we all will get after death, time and space have quite different manifestations. I want to tell you a few cases from my practice that can dispel all doubts about its existence.

Once, I saw a dream about my patient. He came to me after death and began to thank me for the care and support, and said: «How strange - this world is as real as my world. I am not scared. I am surprised. I did not expect this." Waking up and remembering this unusual dream, I thought, «No, how that is possible, I saw him yesterday - he was alright!» But when I came to work, I was told that this patient died the same night. There were no signs of his imminent departure,

so I'm not even thinking about his alleged death, and here - such a strange dream...

Such kind of stories of our patients is a kind of hint for us that life after death does not end, it continues. Moreover, the person who physically dies does not lose his/her memory, because this person can still talk about what the doctor did to him or her, and therefore, he or she is in full consciousness. It tells us that even after physical death, the mind and consciousness remain unchanged. There would not be a new beginning, as a new leaf - without memory, without imagination or what was or what could be.

Summary. *Life after death does not end, but only continues, with unchanged consciousness and feelings.*

Dr. Gnezdilov continues his story.

...Once, there was a woman in our cancer hospital. The forecasts were disappointing - she could not live more than a few weeks. She had a daughter who was a minor, which after her death will be left as an orphan. The woman was really worried about this because the girl will be left all alone. What was waiting for her - a children's home or the street? «My God! Do not let me die now, let me care for my daughter!" - Cried the woman... And in spite of the doctors' predictions, she lived for two years. Apparently, the Lord heard her request and extended her life up to the time when her daughter came of age.

As we can see, she received her plea. Often, our words continue or on the contrary, limits our lives. Even by asking God to give her life in order to see her daughter become of age, a woman with cancer had few more years given to her by God. But if we are afraid of death and do not allow ourselves to think of it as an advantage, we will not be able to see the opportunities and acquisitions from each day lived on here on Earth. The fear of death does not allow us to enjoy life because chances to see opportunities in it are perceived as a threat to life. If you do not appreciate every day of your life, who said that the days and years will be an asset for the future?

Summary. *The fear of death is a kind of restraint, which does not lead to any development, it limits life with just existence and indecision while the value of even a single day we live - is an acquisition for life in Heaven.*

Dr. Gnezdilov continues his story.

We fix death when the heart and the brain stop working. While, at the same time, the death of consciousness - in such a concept, in which it has always been represented - does not exist.

The soul is freed from its shell and clearly aware of the surrounding reality. There are lots of evidence, which are confirmed by the numerous stories of patients who have experienced post-mortem experience in a state of clinical death. Communication with patients is extremely instructive

for us and makes us wonder and wonder because all these extraordinary events simply cannot be attributed to coincidences. These events dispel all doubts about the immortality of our souls. (4)

Life after death is not an accident. If you have thought of death as a restraint on your path, just begin to see it as an opportunity.

Summary. *Death is inevitable; it is something that does not depend on us. But, we can decide how we will see the process of death; As an end or as a beginning of a new life in Heaven?*

Professor of Medicine, Robert Paul Lanza, known for his stem cell research, has his own view on the issue of death.

Our classic way of thinking is based on the belief that the world has an objective existence, independent of the observer. But, many experiments show that it is vice versa. We believe that life is only the activity of carbon and mixtures of molecules: at first we live in, and then rotting in the ground.

After the death of his old friend, Albert Einstein said: «Best left this strange world a little ahead of me. This means nothing. People like us, know that the distinction between past, present, and future is just a stubborn and obsessive illusion.»

Death is an illusion for those who know that the termination of the life of the physical body is not the end but only the beginning. Therefore, for those who do not limit their lives only with terrestrial events, there is no difference between the past and the future, they just continue their life. Even the death of the body will not stop these people in the process of life. It is important to you dear reader to answer the question. Where would you spend eternity? Where will you continue life after death?

We believe in death because we were taught that we die. In addition, of course, because we associate ourselves with our body, and we know that the body will die. End of story. Nevertheless, biocentrism, a new theory, tells us that death cannot be a terminal event as we all think. It's amazing: if you add life and consciousness into the equation, it is possible to explain some of the biggest mysteries of science. For example, it becomes clear why space and time and even the properties of matter itself depend on the observer. It also becomes clear why the laws, constants and the forces of the universe are perfectly matched for life. (5)

Death is just a transition. The transition from something to another thing. You're not afraid to cross the street. Despite the cars, noise and instinct of self-preservation, you still look for the pedestrian crossing for your cross walk. When you know what is waiting for you around the corner, you are not afraid to go there. So what do you actually get from the fear of death if you learn what to expect after death, fear will dissipate by itself because

you will know exactly where your life's decisions will lead you to. There is a common technique used in fairytales that is helpful in choosing the right path, a stone always appears in front of the protagonist on this stone is written: «go right and there you'll get one, but go left there you'll get another.» So, friends, we also have a choice: our life's choices today will present us with two ways in Eternity. The way to Hell, and the way to Heaven. And daily, we make a choice on which way to follow

THE CHOICE BETWEEN LIFE AND DEATH

It is not a revelation that our place of abode after death will be determined by the kind of life we lived here.

Summary. *Whether we like it or not, there will be no choice after death, as well as no excuses.*

The soldier, who was seriously wounded in Vietnam, during surgery, came out of his body and watched as doctors tried to bring him back to life. «*I tried to stop them, because I felt good, where I was at that moment. Certainly, I was there, but he (the doctor), I was not sure whether he was really present there. I grabbed him and he disappeared. I kind of walked through him… And then suddenly, I found myself on the battlefield, where I got this wound. Medics picked*

up the wounded soldiers. I wanted to help them, but suddenly I found myself back in the operating room… I appeared in different places, in the twinkling of an eye…»

These stories inform us that after death, there will be a great amount of truly unique opportunities. We have already mentioned the communication on a telepathic level, and here you have the transferring of information through thoughts or desires. So thoughts can be carried out immediately into action, without the loss of time and the use of special resources. Is it great to get where you want, with the help of your thoughts? These are the advantages of Heaven and they are actually absent during our Earthly life. Are you still afraid to die? Then you are not sure that you will inherit Heaven.

Summary. *Hence, in order to become a part of Heaven, you have to live on Earth not for the body and not for desires but to accept God into your soul and live according to His Word. Not such a difficult task, besides, the benefits of life in Heaven, its beauty, worth it.*

«I heard how the doctor declared that I am dead, and, at this time, it was as if I was floating in some dark space. There are no words to explain it. Everything was completely black, and only far away, I saw the light. It was very bright, but not too big at first, but then, the light was getting bigger and bigger. I wanted this light. I was not scared, I felt good. I am a Christian, and I immediately remembered that, «This light is Christ, as He said:» I am the light of the world.

«I decided that if this is death, then I know what awaits me»

For this guy, death became an advantage. He knows who resides in Heaven, and the bright light is his salvation and his reward. He had no fear of death because he knew exactly what was waiting for him at the end of his life on Earth; a great reward from God, an opportunity to live and enjoy the gifts of Heaven. Based on his story, I want to reaffirm that all who have visited the other side of death saw the light that is uniquely different from what they had seen in real life. But, we are accustomed to asserting that there is nothing better than what we see here. However, it appears that this is not true. All of our Earthly pleasures are but a pale shadow of what we will have in Heaven. That means that the things that you consider as the best today are only amateur copies of a truly fulfilling life. For example, if you have an expensive and a good apartment, it is only a substitute for what is in Heaven. If the Heavens roads are made of gold, what is the value your apartment? Does it stand on a piece of land, clad in asphalt? Just imagine the castle, which is built on jewelry instead of brick, lovely gardens, and trees. The flowers and fruits are of incredible beauty, a type you have never seen or tried. Imagine a waterfall near your house, where drops of flowing water play the music of life, of joy and fun, and the water is not just transparent but is shining with all the colors of the rainbow. Isn't that wonderful? And, we think we've seen a real life, living in the city or village, on your continent.

Summary. *It turns out that life has not yet begun, there is an illusion of visible acquisitions and nothing more.*

«... *I knew that I was dying, and it was impossible to do anything since no one heard me ... I was out of my body, without a doubt, because I saw my body there on the operating table. My soul was outside the body. Because of this, I felt very bad but then appeared this bright light. At first, it was a bit dim, and then, it became like a very bright beam. I could feel the heat from it. The light veils everything but did not prevent me from seeing the operating room, the doctors, nurses, and all the rest. At first, I did not understand what was happening, but then, He sort of asked me if I was ready to die. He spoke like a man, but no one was there. This voice came from the Light.*

Now I think that the Light realized that I'm not ready to die. He seemed to check me. But, from the moment when the light began to speak, I felt very good. I felt that I was in safety and in love. Love, pushed by the Light was unimaginable and indescribable.»(6)

Love this is all that the soldier felt after his death. He had no regrets about his life on Earth or the desire to return. He felt a great love and complete safety. Thus, life after death is not associated with danger, betrayal, envy and disappointments mostly. Living in Heaven is embracing love and eternal pleasure from the fact that you are much loved, and you too love your refuge.

Do you want to conquer your fear of death, or continue to live in fear? It is your own choice. If you know the location of your destination, you will reach your goal. Suppose you are offered a unique chance. For example, a major opportunity at work, which can be a significant contribution to your future. You are going to be paid a million dollars. You are invited to a meeting, and you have to know the address, place, and time. So, you are in the process of preparing, choosing a suit and going to the hairdresser. You are getting ready. But suddenly it turns out that you have not considered the time on the road, have not prepared your route, have not learned and understood the interests of your partners and did not take into account plans and prospects for cooperation. Everything that you previously felt the need to do was to bring your body to the meeting. And without a doubt, you have prepared the body. Even, for example, you took a taxi, not knowing where to go, but were able to find a way out of the situation. Further action is whether you will be offered the same opportunity, and knowing the world of business, and the requirements for business partners, I say: You have failed, partnership won't be possible.

Remember, there is a soul and at some point, the soul leaves the body and the body dies. Where the soul goes depends on your actions today; How you value the time of your life, on what you spend it on, on your body, or for the good of others. Do you learn the route of your possible journey after death? Do you wonder what awaits you next in Heaven or Hell? Do you know the One who created you?

Do you know the main reason of meeting God? Do you know his interests or desires? What are you going to tell Him when you see him? Will He be ready to invite you to live in Heaven with Him? You must carefully consider how you need to live today, and how you can prepare your meeting with God?

Do not live by chance. It is irresponsible and superficial. After all, knowing the course of our journey, we have to act consciously and arm ourselves with knowledge about the place where we're going to. In order not to regret the wrong life, holding the report before God. And, the fact that the Day of Judgment will surely come as also described in the stories of people who have visited Heaven and saw their whole life from beginning to end.

Seneca Sodi
(Paradise, the Holy City and the Glory of God's Throne)

I looked abroad; we were just entering a region of bright clouds something like a glorious, glowing, Earthly sunset, only far superior. The time had been very brief indeed, but we were actually slowing up in the great suburbs of the eternal kingdom.

- Listen a moment, I said to the angel, what music do I hear? Is it real or am I in an imagination?

- *It is the song of the redeemed in Heaven you hear. The entire Heavenly kingdom is full of music without a discord.*

-*No sweeter music ever fell on my ears. I was perfectly enraptured with delight.*

- *Are we near the gates of the city?*

- *Very near to the portals of paradise,» he said. At this, the angels bowed their heads and covered their faces with their hands while I fell flat on my face in the chariot. Stillness reigned in our souls, but deep emotions began to heave in my breast. I felt I must break the silence by shouting the praises of God.*

I sprang to my feet and for a moment seemed perfectly bewildered with what met my gaze in every direction. The light was so transparent and far exceeding perfect day Earth ever afforded.

Clusters of Heavenly flowers were growing everywhere. Groves of beautiful trees loaded with fruit, along with magnificent flowering shrubs beautiful beyond description met my eye in all directions. Roadways like winding streets arranged with exquisite taste and beauty were penetrating this pleasure ground of glory. Lovely souls were coming and going, passing and re-passing each other with the salutations and courtesies that Heaven only knows.

The chariot was now slowing its speed and such raptures

of glory which filled my soul, I cannot describe them! I was simply lost in wonder while I kept saying:

- Surely I am home at last. (1)

The beauty of Heaven is described by a person who saw it with his own eyes, and wondered why he had never seen such a beauty living on Earth. This informs us that the Earth is only a semblance of something more significant, it is just the beginning of our lives, and there is Heaven, where everyone feels at home. There is a proverb which says: «east or west, home is the best.» Hence, we are just guests on Earth. But eternity is our home, where it is always joyful, cozy, and comfortable. Where you feel really secure.

Summary. *If you are not satisfied in life, start thinking about your real home, about Heaven... The fear of death keeps you from forming a true view of Heaven. Live so that death becomes a possibility to acquire a true life after the death of the body.*

To live for eternity means:

To believe that God is the master of your life.

To not entertain any illusions that there is still plenty of time. You have to make a choice in favor of life today.

To love people, be their servant. Not the slave owner selfishly desiring to raise your credibility.

LIFE BEGINS
WHEN WE DIE

«Today, Mary cooked dinner in a special way, telling her husband Leonard, that he would not leave the house because they will have a celebration. Leonard was surprised because there is still a lot of time till his birthday, but knowing his wife's faith in God, he thought: again some Christian holiday, so many of them that he does not actually know when and what. Mary cleaned the house, cooked the favorite soup of her husband, and they began to eat. After the meal, the woman told her husband the following: «today I'm going to die, God will take me. We have lived a good life with you: the children and grandchildren all living, working, they are respected.» Leonard laughed, but seeing the mood of his wife, he realized she was not joking. She helped people daily to overcome the pain of alienation, even relatives.

... In the evening, she lay down on the bed and died. Leonard heard the last breath of her life. «

This story was told by the grandson of that woman. He said that his grandmother was very close to God. She prayed a lot, read the Bible, and served people. This woman lived for the sake of Heaven. She had not limited herself with the fear of death, she was able to defeat it. She conquered death when she decided to become a support for those who were terminally ill. The value of life for her, was in helping other people. With such a close relationship with God, she did not depart from the source of life. She lived and knew exactly when her Earthly journey will be transformed to another form of life. And what had happened to the woman at the time of death is the transition of her soul to another dimension.

In 1907, Dr. Duncan Macdougall, along with his several assistants, decided to weigh dying tuberculosis patients, before and after death. For this, he placed beds with terminally ill patients at the special industrial scales. In each participants of this study he observed a microscopic weight loss immediately after death. It was impossible to explain the difference in the weight with the help of science. Hence, the doctor decided that this slight difference is the weight of the human soul. At the moment of death, the soul leaves the human body and its mass changes accordingly. As a result, scientists announced that the estimated weight of the human soul is 21 grams. He published his results in one of the most respected medical journals.

Immediately after the publication, there were supporters and opponents of the theory. One of the critics immediately noticed that during a person's death, the pelvic muscles relax, and weight loss may be due to the fact that the body is freed from the remnants of urine and feces. This remark was rejected by the doctor, as during the experiment, the bed was weighed with its contents.

Another opponent of the theory said that the loss in weight of the dying may be associated with his last breath. In order to defend his position, a doctor climbed onto the bed

that was standing on the scales and began to breathe the air. At this time, his assistants have closely followed the testimony of weights. There were no changes in weight during exhalation.

The publication continued to attract attention. Eventually, another expert claimed that the human body loses weight due to evaporation of the liquid, of which the human body is made of. Eventually, Dr. Duncan Macdougall reported that the first participant of the experiment lost weight hourly, due to the evaporation of water. The process lasted very slowly, and at the time of the immediate death, weight loss became visible instantly and was exactly 21 grams. (7)

Many of those who were present before the death of an individual, have repeatedly told us that the last thing they can see or hear before the death of this person was a sigh. Many argue that if the soul leaves the body of the dying person, there are barely audible gasp of the dying - so goes the last breathe of life

It turns out that life is a vapor, and in order to conquer the fear of death, we have to understand that life is not the enormous difficulties that we have experienced and it is not the children we raised. Life is a vapor that comes out of the dead body. For example, while in the cold, we breathe and still see the steam that comes from a mix of the outside cold air and our warm breath. Thus, death is the transition of the soul from one state to another.

Summary. *The body dies, but the soul continues to live, and therefore, life goes on, and we need to know, what a true life after death is. If today you do not think about this and hope that «somehow by chance, you will make it by over,» then you're wrong. Remember, to live today is good, but what if life ends tomorrow?*

Life is a vapor, a small cloud, which you cannot see, but easily felt when a person dies. Life is vanity, filled with concerns and opportunities as well, but all these are temporary and fleeting. Now perhaps many recall the phrase of the elderly, who said: «It's as if he did not live at all, the years passed as one brief moment.»

Betty Malz told about her experience of living in a state of clinical death. She traveled across the green hills and the grass was unusually bright green. She was surrounded by colorful flowers, trees, shrubs, and although the sun was not visible, all the space was flooded with bright light. She was accompanied by a tall man in robes, most likely, an angel. Together they approached the silver structure, similar to the palace. Around was heard the melodious singing of the harmonious chorus of voices.

It seems that the woman telling her vision of Heaven, speaks of Earthly forms. Trees, green hills, flowers, and shrubs all around it is a hint for us: Heaven is a prototype of the Earth, which means that everything that we see and what we use on Earth is the same in Heaven. However, amazing details of «unusually vivid colors» say that people

find it difficult to convey the beauty of colors, because, previously, they have never seen such saturated colors. «Colorful Flowers» is also a spectacle of inexpressible beauty, how else can you describe what you see for the first time? All this is in the Heavens and here, we just see it in the form of copies of a lower quality. For example, the roses are only a likeness of the flowers that are in Heaven. How about such possibilities? And,we think that living on Earth has its advantages …

Before them, there was a gate. About four meters high, made of pearl leaf. The angel touched them, and they opened. Inside, there was a street of a gold color. Inside there was a blinding bright yellow light. She felt the presence of someone, and Betty knew that it was Jesus. The woman was invited to enter, but then she thought about her father who prayed for her.

A hint for us that memory remains as it was before death. Consciousness is in full working order, and therefore, we would feel both joy and pain. Please, you cannot go to Hell; you cannot afford to feel pain in eternity because of your pride and thought that Heaven and Hell are a fiction.

The gate slammed shut, the woman began to descend the hill, just seeing the light on the wall that was covered with jewels.

It is no coincidence that women love jewelry, everything comes from Heaven where God the Creator

is waiting for his children. Here, we can see only a shadow of what awaits us in Heaven. Here, in order to obtain something, you need to work, to work hard, but in Heaven, it's all there in abundance in order to please precious children.

Heaven is so beautiful that everyone who had the opportunity to be there came back into his or her body with a great regret. And, we are afraid of death, thinking that this is the end. But, it is easy to overcome the fear of death for the person who decides to live at a higher level, who has not limited his life, who will be able to see and imagine the beauty of Heaven. We see our life on Earth and think that this is the ultimate dream. But, reading stories about people who have been in Heaven, and who did not want to return, because of the beauty, we can conclude that there is something more attractive for life in Heaven, something which you do not want to refuse.

Summary. *It can be stated that life on Earth is not the limit of our dreams. We think of how good it is to live here, as if there is no better place for living, but it turns out that we just have not seen anything better.*

BE READY TO DIE

The body in which we are born, is not life itself, but rather a place that should be filled with life. If the body is not filled with life, it is not living, that is why there is the birth of a stillborn child when the fetus dies in the womb. There is no soul, the main component for the body to live. It also happens when a person is in coma: here is the body, organs are working, but there is no life, no soul. Therefore, our body is not life itself, there is a room for something, namely for the soul. Then why is everyone so afraid of death of the body?

Summary. *Death is the rejection of your body, which, over the years, becomes weak and can later become a burden.*

Being prepared to die does not mean to just sit and wait for something. Be prepared to die, means to realize that you really are going to Heaven. It means that you have defined your way of life and taught the people around you to live for the benefit of others.

To release the fear of death means:

To know your destination for eternity, and to live in such a way to ensure that you have done everything possible for God and people.

Not to be proud of your temporary successes, to live as if you have done nothing at all.

To ask God for strength and his love to enable you live not for yourself, but for others, pointing them to the way to Heaven.

In order to make the first move in favor of the choice of life in Heaven, you have to accept God into your soul and realize that you are not the master of your fate, but the Lord, who gave you life on Earth with one desire: that you may inherit Heaven.

There is one moment from atheism to God!
One moment in annihilation's waste,
One moment, of the well of life to taste -
The stars are setting, and the Caravan
Starts for the dawn of Nothing – Oh, make haste!

Omar Khayyam,
(Persian poet & writer, philosopher, mathematician)

Saying that the soul exists, it is necessary to reflect on the fact that leaving the body, it has to go somewhere. Do not think that the point of destination is situated on the Planet of Apes. Do not think that the most important thing is to spend your life here on Earth, and it does not matter what will happen after death. On the contrary, it is important what comes after life on Earth.

Summary. *Earth is a place of temporary stay while Heaven is the permanence.* Therefore, it is important to know where your permanent place of residence will be after a temporary life on Earth. It is important today to understand and find the answer, where will you spend eternity in Heaven or in Hell?

It should also be understood that in addition to Heaven there is also Hell. This is the place, where some souls of people are sent, those not reconciled with God, and did not live according to His word and His will. Therefore, you now need to ask yourself one question: «Where do I want to spend my eternity, in Heaven or in Hell?» If our choice is Heaven, then it is necessary to live according to the law of Eternity. You may ask, how can I resist the urge to gain the whole world and loose my soul? You must therefore live having a total control of your desires. This is what it means not to live fully.

Summary. *Life is full when it is led by you, by your mind and not your desires, emotions, or the influence of friends.* It is also clear that life on Earth is measured in years, and for someone it may be 85 years, for another 45 years, and the third it is 25 years, but life after death is measured in eternity. It does not have a temporary space and it cannot be measured by years, days, or hours. It is a never-ending stream of time.

Do you want to enjoy a short-term fad of life on Earth? It is your right if that is your desire, and the responsibility

and consequences for this choice is totally on you. You will have no one to blame but yourself, as you make every decision. But, what will happen after death in Heaven, you can see by reading this book. The fear of death can be easily defeated, if you do not just learn what Heaven looks like, but in all your deeds put into practice all you have studied.

Who knows, if to live is to be dead, and to be dead to live?

Euripides,
(Ancient Greek dramatist)

Euripides perfectly noticed the wisdom of human perception. After all, we do not really know what our true acquisition is; life or death. Nevertheless, we do know one thing: life on Earth is like death, but the death of the body will be our real life if we make a choice in favor of Heaven.

You will make a choice in favor of life after death if you can see the benefits of Heaven. The ignorance about the beauty of life in Heaven can be compared with the fact that you for example, heard a lot about movies in 4D format but have never seen them. However, when you feel the whole range of emotions, you will be impressed, watching this film in this format. This is because you try what many have heard, but not seen. To see the benefits is to imagine Heaven for yourself and realize that you will inherit it by living a decent life on Earth.

Those people who accepted God and served people, are aware of the advantages of death. They know exactly that the Creator is waiting for them in Heaven.

The famous preacher Tommy Lee Osborn died on February 14, in his ninetieth year of life. He died at home, surrounded by family. Before his death, he turned to the Lord and said, «Take me home.»

Here is what his daughter said.

On this day, my father gathered the children and said, «I will ask Jesus to pick me up. I am more than ninety years, I do not want to live, I have done my job, and I am tired. My wife is already there, and I go home to Daisy, she is waiting for me". The next day he asked Jesus about the same, referring to his eternal home, to a meeting with Jesus, and then, he was just gone.

You may ask why this man was so sure that he was going to Heaven, where did he get such a belief and confidence. He was absolutely not afraid of death; he defeated the fear of death by his confidence in life in Heaven. So often we are afraid, we do not want to go to Heaven because we are afraid of death. Being in a hospital, we feel the fear that life can end. But I have to inform you that indeed, someday, your life will end. Tommy Lee was not afraid of death, as he was confident that he was going home to Heaven, for one simple reason: he believed in the Word, which says: «The will of my Father, is to see the son that whoever believes in Him will inherit eternal life.» He knew that he would not die, it was his life. He was not afraid because he knew that life is the path, and this path does not end here. He saw the continuation of a real life in Heaven, defeating the fear of death by his faith in eternity. For us to have the opportunity, we must:

1. Believe in Jesus Christ. Because our salvation cannot be obtained by money and it is not just enough to do good things. The Bible says: «Everyone who believes in Him, inherits eternal life.» Please note that eternal life is not acquired only by good deeds, but by faith in the Son, Jesus Christ.

2. Serve other people. It is important to be there for people who need our help. This means to live not only for our own concerns, business, or needs. But to seek out and help those who need words of support, guidance, substance or clothing.

Tommy Lee was fifteen years old when God called him to become a preacher. In 1939, after finishing eighth grade, Osborne began to help one evangelist; he was responsible for hosting the youth evenings.

Osborne knew that God loved him, and He has a plan for the life of the young man. Hence, he had changed his attitude toward the ministry he just wanted to glorify Christ. Since that time, God's miracles and healing were manifested through the ministry of the Osborne family.

From 1950 to 1964 the family traveled to forty countries, preaching the Gospel and carrying out the healing ministry. Osborne family was supported by thirty-thousand pastors and helped to spread the Gospel in the fifty-thousand villages in Thailand.

Their books have been published in 132 languages. Videos of ministries, in which God revealed miracles, is translated into 67 languages. (8)

Life is predictable, especially for the people who know what the meaning of life on Earth is.

Summary. *People, who are living for others, and help not only their families but make every effort to help other people, live for God and know him very closely.* You can make a comparison with our parents: we may not meet with them every day, but we still know who they are.

In concluding this chapter, I want to say that one of the main ideas which each of us knows for sure is that there is something inevitable in our lives and it is the death of our body. But few people think about what's coming next, after death. My advice: do not wait for an opportunity to find answers to these questions, look for them today to get rid of the fear of death and live on Earth for eternity. Read this book and determine to answer the questions about what will happen after your death. According to Andrew Sachs, a British actor, «**Death is far universal than life. Everyone dies, but not everyone lives.**»

In the next chapter, we will talk about how to inherit Heaven after death. Many people mistakenly think that no one can, just as many think that they will without making preparations. To clarify, we'll talk about it, relying on the truth from The Holy Bible.

Well, let us make some Summaries about the main results of this chapter.

Death does not ask us when it should come. We must be prepared knowing that sooner or later it will happen to us. But, the way we perceive this process determines whether we will live fully until death.

Each of us is given the chance to live today, and our goal is to live in such a way, to be able to go to Heaven. The one who lives only with their concerns will see this possibility only after death when it will be too late to change anything. We need to know the beauty of Heaven and aim at life in Eternity while being on Earth.

The soul is a life that changes its location. Hence, we have a choice: to strive for life in Heaven or agree with our habits and spend eternity in Hell. We have to make this choice today, to live every day for eternity, overcoming the fear of death every day.

Do not expect that your good deeds will provide you with a ticket to Heaven. The fundamental and significant condition is to accept Jesus Christ as your Lord and Savior.

To put Him first and ask for the forgiveness for your sins. Serving people should be your way of life but remember, without the first condition, your good deeds are in vain.

GOLDEN TRUTH

• Death is stronger than life, and there is no one who would not die.

• Do not think that you can live the way you want, you have to live the way you should.

• Life was given to us by the Creator, and you rent it for a certain period of time.

• The limitations of our knowledge do not allow us to be ready for a lot of things and events in our lives, and especially for death.

• Life is like a small cloud, which you cannot see, but it easy to feel when the person dies.

• Today we must prepare for a major meeting in our short life. The meeting with God, the Creator of our life.

• Life on Earth is not the limit of our dreams.

• Life is full when it is led directly by you, by your mind, and not by your desires, emotions, and the influence of friends.

• People, who live in the name of others, who help not only their family but do everything possible to help others, live for God.

• Death is far universal than life because everyone dies, but not everyone lives.

TEST
"FEAR HAS
A HUNDRED EYES"

In each statement or question of the test, there should be only one answer. Next to each answer, in brackets, is a score. Your result of the test corresponds to the obtained amount of points.

1. Are you afraid to die today? Why?
a) Yes, of course. (0)
b) Yes, I'm still young. (1)
c) I have not thought about this before. (1)
d) I do not think I'm afraid, but I understand that I lived for myself. (2)
e) No, I live for other people. (3)

2. What does it mean to be ready for death?
a) To live to old age. (0)
b) To write a will. (1)
c) To live life well, without sins. (2)
d) To live for other people, while appreciating every day of my life. (3)

3. What do you know about the soul?
a) The soul is my desire. (1)
b) It is not interesting for me. (0)
c) The soul is continuously reincarnated. (1)
d) The soul is life. (3)

4. Advantages of death?
   a) There are no benefits, there is only fear. (0)
   b) No advantage exists, only grief. (1)
   c) The ability to see something new, unknown
      to anyone. (2)
   d) To live in Heaven for eternity. (3)

5. What will happen to you after death?
   a) Funeral. (0)
   b) I will be the subject of reincarnation in
      another life. (1)
   c) The judgment of God. (2)
   d) A new life. (3)

RESULTS
OF THE TEST

0-5 points. You do not ask important questions of life after death. You live your life just for successful events. But you must consider where you want to spend eternity and it is also worth noting that there is more to life than satisfying your own desires.

6-9 points. You know that life is not eternal, but you adhere to your beliefs because you avoid responsibility. After all, to accept God as the Creator of life would be to change your lifestyle. Reading the book, you will understand how you can change your beliefs and a great opportunity to live fully.

10-15 points. You enjoy life on Earth, having a clear idea of what awaits you in Heaven. You made a report of every single day and you are guided by an aim; to please the Lord. You live every day with a desire to be complete here on Earth and to see the beauty of Heaven.

PRACTICAL
TASKS

1. What evokes fear in you, causing you to fear death? State the actions you still blame yourself for?

2. Are you willing to forgive yourself right now? Write a letter to yourself with the words of forgiveness, stating the things you are ready to forgive in yourself.

3. How do you plan to amend your ways so as to live in view of Heaven? Write down three things you do daily to be able to live in Heaven.

4. Write down at least three decisions that you made, while reading this chapter.

Having formed the necessary qualities that exude good character, you will be able to gather the pieces from various experiences to give you the big picture of what life is all about.

Chapter 2

SO, WHO GOES TO HEAVEN

Chapter 2
SO, WHO GOES
TO HEAVEN

It is sad to talk about death, but in the last chapter, we saw that death is just a transition that allows us to gain an eternity either in Heaven or in Hell. Therefore, to avoid self-judgment, or not to form a new fear of uncertainty about where you would spend eternity we will focus on the opportunity to get an eternity in Heaven immediately. I'll tell you with excitement that every person in the world has this opportunity from God.

THERE ARE NO CHOSEN PEOPLE

For it is by grace you have been saved, through faith— and this is not from yourselves, it is the gift of God— not by works so that no one can boast.

Ephesians 2:8

The Apostle Paul conveyed this message from God to the people. Once again informing us that we are saved by the grace of God, by His great love for us. We do not decide and we do not know, who will be saved and who will not. After all, many of us do not know how people encounter

God, form and build their relationship with Him. So, people cannot decide who is worthy and who is not, just as you cannot get salvation from money or good deeds. Salvation is God's greatest gift to us.

We will answer the main questions of this chapter together, «So, who goes to Heaven?»

1. Eternity in Heaven is inherited by a person who KNOWS Jesus Christ as Lord and Savior. This is not the kind of person who casually hears about Jesus, not the one who attends a church service. Not the one who lighted a candle in church or participated in a fast. And not even the one who has ever uttered a prayer of repentance, acknowledging Jesus Christ as Savior. But the one who knows Jesus personally, who sought for Him in sincerity of the heart, and found Him as the most precious thing in life. This is a person who tells God about his exploits and falls, who seeks Him through the knowledge of the Word of God, who lives life with His love and knows that Jesus had done the same for him. Such a person may not be a member of a church, attended great services, but he knows Christ personally.

2. Eternity in Heaven is inherited by the person who made Jesus a friend while on Earth. These are the people who defended the position of Christ, and every day of their lives sought to know Him not only as God but also as a friend. When we make friends, we want to communicate with them, , we strive to meet them, support, and help

with everything we have. Many people who were beside Him, next to Him were such friends to Jesus. They walked with Him from village to village, and from town to town. Thanks to their loyalty, they had the opportunity to learn from him. A friend is a person who will never betray you.

3. The one who will go to Heaven will not just be a friend of God but will also walk with God. An example for us is the life of the Apostles or the prophets who were on Earth, for example, Peter and Abraham. It does not mean that they were perfect. They did not just serve the Lord, nor just prophesied or preached. They walked with God, they heard God's heartbeat. They lived His dreams, His thoughts and His words. Their only priority was to walk with God.

4. The person who lives for God every day inherits eternity. Paul a perfect example, he was living his life in a way he did not want, but later encountered the Lord Jesus Christ and went ahead to live for the purpose of God, he fulfilled His task, he lived only for Christ. Living for God does not mean visiting services only on Sundays; it does not mean to serve in the church. It means to fulfill the purpose of Jesus Christ daily.

5. The one who will become a resident of Heaven will make the Lord the master of their life. This person consciously refuses to live for self, they devote themselves to Godly service because He is the master of their life. This person voluntarily becomes a slave of God and deprives self of everything. They abandon their path, intentions

and desires giving themselves to God, understanding that «The Lord is the master, and nothing is theirs.»

As you can see from these points, the principle is just one: for anyone to inherit Heaven, the most important criteria is to build a relationship with God. Often, we tell ourselves that sin separates us from the Father, but the point is that sin **does not drag people to Hell, but the lack of relationship with the Savior.** Sin may affect this relationship with the Father. We have a choice: to build this relationship, by taking the sacrificial love of Christ, or give up this relationship and live as we desire.

Many of us live thinking that our life is measured in days or years. However, death will not ask, warn or inform anyone of the moment it will come to interrupt life. In order to become a person who will live with God in Heaven, a personal relationship with Jesus is prescribed. We need to abandon the fears and false beliefs, tell ourselves that we will not let anyone steal our relationship with God - neither the circumstances of life nor the fear of death, nor our superficial belief in salvation with the help of Jesus Christ.

Ask yourself one question: «Am I afraid to die?» take a break and admit to yourself honestly, Is this a fear in your life? Talking about the superficial faith, I want to convey the idea that if in your life there is the fear of death; it says that you are not sure that after death you will gain eternal life. Looking at your way of life, the thoughts, words, and actions, you do not believe that God will allow them

in Heaven. This lack of confidence is based on a lack of understanding of your relationship with our Savior, Jesus Christ.

Summary. *You need your faith in life and dedication to the knowledge of Jesus Christ as his friend to defeat the fear of death.*

Sometimes, we judge people based on their considerations. A good man or not, beautiful or not, according to their behavior in relation to others. We define favorites for ourselves. Those with whom we are friends, accept, help, and reject those who are not like us – poorly educated, lower class in the society. We are trying to build our surroundings based on such convictions. However, more than that, we are trying to create faith in God because of such an attitude towards people. This is an issue why many Christians do not live fully in joy, and faith that would provide full assurance of their salvation. Because we gain salvation from how we will build our communication with God. It is important to understand that when we are talking about the relationship with people, it is:

1. The desire to see people through the eyes of God

2. To have no fear to engage in a heart-to-heart conversation

3. The ability to share their successes and failures

4. To Love without expectations

5. To seek to know the person more

~ 74 ~

These principles of relations are acceptable between people, as well as between God and a human. Therefore, we should aspire to have these points effective in our lives while building our relationship with God. Often, people are turning to God when things are bad; there is a Ukrainian proverb which says that: «When danger passes, God is forgotten» in other words, when things are bad, we hurry to know Him and get an answer, but when all is well, we do not need the Lord anymore. This is an attitude of a consumer and God is not delighted with it and therefore no personal relationship is built with God.

A supernatural environment is not required to build a relationship with God. For God who created the Earth, there is no separation of people: there are no «special» people, whom he loves, and «ordinary» people whom He doesn't and they simply exist. There are no favorites and outcasts, no special or insignificant people for God who gave us life. The very fact that you have a life defines His love for you. Life, for us, is a gift from God, and it is in everyone who lives today or is born today, it is a special stamp of exclusivity from God. Everything else is a special love; the exclusivity depends on how you or I know the Lord as our Savior at this period in life. The way we know God formed our level of faith when initially we just know him personally, and eventually give our lives in His hands, saying, «Nothing is mine.»

We think that the love of God must be earned, but it is a misconception: we do not receive love from our great

deeds, or talents, or good intentions, but because it exists. To know how much God loves you, you need to remember how much you have experienced in your life because of His love, thanks to special occasions, which always stand after His love. This is the first step of the belief that Jesus did not die for the sake of someone's greatness, that he was the most special, or the most beloved. It was because His love for mankind was far above all. Moreover, what needs to be special is to understand that our lives are special because of His love and our salvation is His sacrificial love for us.

Summary. *There are no such people who do not deserve eternity in Heaven; there are only those who do not want to come closer to the Lord.*

Therefore, if you still value your contribution in life, counting all your good deeds and evaluating your self-worth, then stop doing it. All that is needed is to accept Jesus Christ as your Lord and Savior, and develop a personal relationship with Him by believing in your salvation and seeking to know Him more daily.

There is a wonderful parable about being called and chosen in the Bible. It talks about people around us, who invite us to the banquet of our Heavenly Father, but we reject it offensively, and laugh at them, saying that they are abnormal. At that moment, when we refuse, we are losing a way to salvation; we lose faith in our eternity. However, there are those who accept the calling, there are those who trust their lives, not to themselves, but to the Lord, saying:

«Who am I, without you, my Lord.» The Lord calls such people favorites. This is not because He had chosen them, but because many people are called through the word of faith, through the call to salvation, through the story of the sacrifice of Jesus Christ but few are chosen. So, when a person receives God's call, he becomes chosen.

So do not think that God chooses people by Himself. He does not say that one is right for me and the other one is not. It depends on us whether we accept Him in our lives, whether we live for Him and if we know Him personally.

Summary. *We need to take a position of choosing for ourselves to defeat the fear of death remembering that God loves us.* Even if today you do not make a choice to accept Jesus. He will continue to wait, to love and to forgive whenever you approach Him.

YOU ARE ALWAYS MINE
Rosalia Marchenko

I washed you from the dirt,
Washed the soot away from your face.
I rubbed the ointment on the scabs,
So, you were not the same.
I cleaned your body,
Dress-White put.
My heart was singing,
By preparing your destiny.

I made your tresses,
Gave you the crown.
Wash your dew
And again you become like nobody else.
But then something changed,
You're leaving.
My dear suddenly disappeared
And left me.
Your heart is waxed gross,
You went to the other gods.
Slamming the door of the heart,
Attentive to their feet.
I've been waiting, waiting,
You will come back.
About you only remembering
Emptied your garden in the soul.
As the vine, the holy seed,
Put you in the garden.
But after all,
You are going on the same way.
Here you are going to meet me,
Darling, you are mine.
I stretch out his hands, crying...
I still do not have you.
White dress was torn,
Mess entire hem,
And they stole the crown
Mocked you.
Tearing body,
Abused you.

Idol has done his job,
Kicked you by his leg.
But I will justify you.
Holiness will return to you.
And treason forget
You're mine, come to me!

✳ ✳ ✳

Whatever is happening in your life. Do not look for comfort in people, do not look for the answer in the circumstance, come to God and ask for forgiveness, he will take you back. He is waiting.

Summary. *Be mindful of God's unconditional love, because the grace of knowing Jesus Christ comes through it and always remember to walk before God.* We gain eternity in Heaven, when we go to God seeking His purposes for our life, and asking Him for the ability to fulfill all He has committed into our hands.

BELIEF IN ETERNITY

Those who hope for no other life are dead even for this.
Johann Wolfgang Goethe

(German writer and statesman)

Each person has the right to choose; to believe or not to believe. But, the one who has no idea in what to believe does not use this right. Most people live without thinking about what will happen after their death. As Goethe stated, if we do not believe in a future life, then we are dead to the present life. It turns out that without defeating the fear of death, we live scared, fearing the loss of our body. Fear of death is inherent to those who have no confidence in their tomorrow, who do not know what to expect from life, who do not know what to expect around the corner of an unfamiliar street, who are not sure whether they have enough money to live until the next paycheck. All these trivial concerns are based on one fact - lack of faith.

Jesus Christ said something that clarified the meaning of faith. Faith is not something you can buy or find, it is what you believe. «According to your faith be it unto you.» We get in our life what we believe in. If you tell yourself every day that there is no God and you are convinced you are an atheist, it is exactly what you believe in and you will pay for this at the end of your life on Earth. You cannot buy eternity in Heaven; you will not see the beauty and greatness of God because you did not believe. As we know that eternity is so close and does not depend on deeds, but on the sincerity of the heart, you should use this to confess your love for God.

Maybe you are afraid of being convicted for your faith, and, therefore, do not go to church, or you are afraid to be persecuted for your love of Christ and, therefore, live in

fear, but who says that you are not worthy of eternity? Here is how a publican and later the Apostle Matthew wrote at that point: «*But when you pray, go into your room, close the door and pray to your Father, who is unseen. Then your Father, who sees what is done in secret, will reward you.*» Do not wait for favorable conditions, do not be afraid to be unaccepted by people, form your own relationship with God: it is the only key to your salvation.

Perhaps you are saying that you are great and your business speaks for you, or you simply believe that you live righteously somewhere deep in your heart, without obvious sins. I have to disappoint you: the belief in eternity and the acquisition of eternal life does not depend on your affairs; it is based only on your relationship with God and how well you know Him. Returning to the words of the Apostle Paul, we are obliged to keep and remember this opportunity in the acquisition of salvation. This is not the merit or our identity, or the special love of God, but it is an opportunity from God and all that is needed is to use it: «*For it is by grace you have been saved, through faith—and this is not from yourselves, it is the gift of God-not by works, so that no one can boast.*»

We are saved! Faith doesn't depend on our works or serving. It is given to us as a gift, a gift from God. Let's illustrate this gift of salvation with a life example, to see the value of this acquisition and to understand how foolish and stupid we behave in life after receiving the gift.

Imagine you are sailing on a raft, and suddenly a storm and strong wind starts rising, carrying you out to sea, and you realize that you are drowning. You are floundering and trying to swim, but the chances are very big that death is inevitable. Your powerlessness makes itself known, and you start to sink. However, a boat suddenly appears next to you and the people on board rescue you. The water is pumped out of your lungs, bringing you back to life. You are saved. The first thing you probably will do as a human being is to thank those who saved you, helped you and returned your life. In addition, I think it is unlikely you would be as careless as before, and certainly, you will keep a safe position on the ship, clutching the railing and holding fast on your feet. However, imagine that you came to your senses and began telling everyone about your experiences, that you have been saved because you are exceptional, and you return to living again in the pleasure that almost destroyed you, and you do not care about what happened. You will celebrate your heroism and pride while finding yourself again in the sea with probably no one to save you.

So, this story illustrates the fact that salvation is not by merit or strength. It is not acquired as a gift from man, nor of self, but from God. I'll hold on to Him with everything that I have. I will not praise myself, my life and my deeds. I will always realize that there is nothing which I need to hold on, and that salvation is not by works. It is only the Lord whom I hold on to, it is him I value. This is what will ensure my salvation, which can be maintained in any life storm.

Summary. *The one who holds on to God with all strength and all faith will secure the salvation given to us as a gift.*

When a child is born, the parents begin to plan what kind of life they will give him: The Mother can dream about what kindergarten to send her child, what friends he will have. Father can draw a picture of how he will drive the child to school, form a love for cars or for football in his child. However, the most important gift that the Father of our lives gives us is the gift of salvation that we cannot buy with money. The gift that cannot be deserved because of our behavior or obedience. A gift that is not transferred due to any special heritage or because someone is His favorite, but is given by God to everyone who believes in the salvation through the sacrifice of Jesus Christ, and recognized Him as their Lord and Savior.

Therefore, if you are a servant and you can see that you do not get everything today, never doubt in your salvation. Today, if you are condemning yourself because you do not have the time or the opportunity to attend church do not lose your salvation. If today you have sinned, and feel that you cannot be forgiven, and you cannot be chosen, do not give up your salvation to lies. ***Salvation is not something we earned, it is a free gift.***Salvation is not an agreement with the circumstances that may destroy or crush your life. Salvation is not condemnation or disappointment that you could not do more or better for God. Salvation is the gift that enables us enjoy a relationship with God. Salvation

is the confidence that you love and know the Lord personally as a Friend and a Father. It is a decision to live with the faith in your salvation until the last breath of your life and disagree with the sinful nature of your flesh.

The only thing that can steal your salvation and eternity in Heaven is sin. Nothing can separate you from the love of the Father, no far-fetched condemnation, frustration, or fall, only your impotence, and acceptance of sin. When you agree with sin and let it affect your relationship with God. It separates you from Him. Well, we'll talk about this more in subsequent chapters.

WE INHERIT ETERNAL LIFE NOT BY OUR WORKS BUT THROUGH OUR RELATIONSHIP WITH GOD

Not the great deeds are dear to God, but the great love with which they are made.

Saint Basil the Great

Serge is the labor teacher in a secondary school. It seems to be an unremarkable profession that is not particularly popular common among students. But, the kids love his lessons and high school students are not skipping them. This teacher, who rarely attended a training course, learnt something more by the fact that one meeting changed his life.

Arrived on vacation, Serge's daughter shared the news of God's love that God with him. She brought the Bible to her father and asked for permission to pray for him, and expressed her gratitude to allow her share with him. All holidays they read the Bible together and talked about Jesus Christ, who took upon Himself the sins of the world, and that through faith in Him we get comfort and eternity. His daughter's vacation ended, but Serge's life just begun. Though in the village there was no church, which his daughter could visit. He did not start the day without a word of thanksgiving to God, and he ended the evening with stories about children who made the decision to serve God.

He learned to love and appreciate something more in students than just a part of the educational system. He sees a person full of talents and characteristics that he voiced to everyone who comes into contact with him. He does not follow the planned work but teaches according to the purity of his love to God and to the people with whom he works.

In summary, I want to say that no great deed or service will determine how much God loves us. Neither the number of people who learn about us through our word of salvation, but our relationship with God will say more about us than deeds. Because we will fulfill God's will as we will know it more. Since God's value is his love for people; therefore, it should be our value. The value of God - is forgiveness, and therefore, it will be our value. You will be able to see how it will change your life and relationships with people by building a relationship with God.

Our attitude to salvation depends on how close we are to God. Often, we are guided by our desires, our attitude to life and personal benefits. But, all this is in vain if we do not have a relationship with God, from whom we receive the ability to love, to give happiness and to rejoice even in daunting circumstances.

Only one has no sin,
who was not born, and has not lived!

Valery Denisov,
(Soviet and Russian circus performer)

If we live, if we were born, then, we are already sinful, but the essence of salvation doesn't stop us from striving for holiness. Sin - is just an opportunity to realize that we are human beings and that not everything can go on our own will this life. From the standpoint of Christianity, a sin is an act that violates the precepts of God. Therefore, it is impossible to say that there is someone who does not commit sin. But going back to the answer on the question of who will still go to Heaven, we do not come to the summary that it is saints and blameless people. We realized that it is the one who knows God, builds a relationship with Him, seeks not for their own, but gave their life to Him.

Sin can take place on our Earthly path, but it should not become a way of life. One person came to me during my consultation for advice on how to get rid of his bad habit of smoking. I then proceeded to ask him questions

relating to his lifestyle. His answer was ambiguous: he wanted to get rid of this habit, but the love of smoking made it impossible to give it up. When we talked, he had regret about his actions, but at the same time, it was evident that he couldn't deny himself the pleasure.

Summary. *Sin is a conscious decision not to deny yourself pleasure.* It turns out that the scales are still outweighed by the love of this habit in the case of servitude. It seems there is a resistance to sin, but flesh and self-pity are much higher than personal salvation. However, this does not mean that such a person has no chance for salvation. All that is needed is to not rely on themselves, and rush into the secret room with God and ask Him for strength to overcome the weaknesses.

We often see a situation where people hear about a church, but do not want to join it because of the fact that it will deny them there usual way of life. However, tell me, has alcohol made anyone healthier, has smoking really brought joy to people? Nevertheless, we do not want to change, thinking that by rooting out bad habits, we will lose the meaning of life. However, our habits steal our time and life itself. So if you have a fear of death, reconsider your habits, maybe you should give them up for a life that does not end up hell, but for one that will continue in Heaven.

Sin is part of our lives, and we do not notice sometimes how we treat ourselves, God and people around us. Moreover, when there is no line between sin and holiness,

when we agree with what is happening, how we live is quietly, but very quickly becomes part of our lives. We kill people in our thoughts, emotions, and reactions, but we say that we are righteous, we do not give a report of our actions, especially those nobody can see except us. It is good when someone notices an obvious sin, such as drunken or aggressive behavior, but there are those personal sins that we carry in our thoughts, hypocritically playing a double role. When we cease to fight for our holiness, we lose our gift of salvation, taking the sin which is much closer to our lifestyle.

There are those who sin, but do not remain in it, they desire to please the Lord, so every day of their life, they strive to remain holy. This lifestyle is acquired through repentance and a personal relationship with God. As long as we struggle we live.

Summary. *If there is a sin, it has to be defeated with your love for God, with an everyday desire to give up sin and live for God.* How to determine if you are living in sin. He lives in sin:

Who does not repent and deny sin

Who does not wish to give up the traditional way of life and does not want to control their desires

Who does not see its effect, even when others talk about it

Who is eager to please the flesh and its desires and does not resist it

Who takes sin as a karma and accepts it

Who loves sin and does not understand how to deny it

Who depends on sin and repeats it again and again

Often, we hear young people say: «In life, you need to try everything.» Such lifestyle leads to the fact that eventually they become a hostage of their sin, and their life is ruled not by themselves, but their sin. When it comes to a clear awareness that this is bad and harmful to their health, and to life itself, but there is no strength to refuse the satisfaction of sin. There is no strength just because of reliance on self, but who you are, even if your appearance is determined not by you. The strength we find when we come to Jesus as a friend and say that we need help that is what we do in life when we face challenges. We hurry to family and friends to ask for their help. The closest and most faithful isn't our family and friends but only God. The life that we have is from God, the salvation that we acquire is a gift from God. The belief in the salvation is from His great love, it doesn't matter how good we are. *Whatever happens in your life, the most important thing will be your relationship with God.*

I will also discuss with you in this chapter, the scripture which helps form the faith of many Christian's salvation.

Many people can start their Christian journey in a great way, but it will always be important, how we go through it. In the book of Proverbs written by a wise King; Solomon, there is a verse which says: *«For a righteous man falls seven times and rises again.»* This tells us that we will suffer trials, temptations and difficulties on our path of life. However, if we know God personally nothing will steal our salvation. The fall is inevitable in our lives, but it is not important how we fall, the important thing is how quickly we are able to rise and move on thanks to our loyalty to God. *The righteous is such not because they fell or went through any tests, but because they were able to overcome it.* The righteous does not allow self-pity in their path when they fall, they are motivated by the love of God, and being mindful of this love enables them rise again. What a great love, a love that only comes from the person of Jesus Christ. Our Heavenly Father loves each of us before we were born, this truth must be much more valuable to you in your life, much more valuable than the fear of death and much more valuable than sin, to which you are facing. No matter what you think about yourself, whether you are judging or forgiving yourself, it is important that God forgives you when you come to him, no matter what. All that is necessary for each of us - is not to agree with the sin, never reuniting with it or allowing it to be the usual way of life. We must understand that God looks at our heart and waits. He waits for us to come and say, «Father, forgive me.» Your sincere repentance should melt the wall between you and God, which was built by sin.

Thus, the place to spend eternity does not depend on good deeds but on the relationships built with people and the Lord. All He needs from us is our relationship with Him and our desire to know Him as a Father, to love Him more than anyone in our lives. Eternity is open to every person, for everyone who seeks to know the Heavenly Father and to build a quality relationship with Him.

Let's summarize this section and define the key points for our lives.

Good deeds will not bring you closer to eternity without a sincere relationship with God. You cannot buy Heaven with your status or the amount of good deeds you have done. The only thing that is your way to eternity is a sincere relationship with Jesus Christ. This is the main criterion that will give you the strength to always strive for holiness.

God is impartial, He did not select special people, and He does not have favorites. Salvation is His gift to us. Every person is valuable and expensive in His sight. We are not saved by works, but by the sincerity of our hearts. However, we often neglect this, condemning ourselves, thinking that we are not worthy. We must not give up. And we must remember that salvation is acquired when we accept Jesus Christ as our Lord and Savior.

All we need for our salvation and eternity is to believe and hold on to our salvation. It is through salvation we gain

eternal life. Moreover, we should know that after death we are not waiting for Hell, we definitely defeat the fear of death in our life. How can we be afraid of what will be our access to eternal life?

Sin is a process, and we have the power to resist it. Anyone who does not accept sin and refuses to live with it, is fully fighting for his holiness, and, therefore, tends to please God and not themselves. It is not important how you fall, it is important how quickly you rise and go further along the path of life.

Later in this book we will talk about the simple conditions that will help us to get to Heaven. Though these conditions are available, we still live with the wrong priorities, fooling ourselves and thinking that death is the end of everything in our lives. First, let us read the Undeniable truth of this chapter.

GOLDEN TRUTH

• Everyone living on Earth has the opportunity to spend eternity in Heaven with God

• Eternity in Heaven is inherited by the person who KNOWS Jesus Christ as Lord and Savior

• The one who will become a resident of Heaven will make the Lord the master of his life

• Out do yourself to win your lifestyle, to abandon the fears, false beliefs, and tell yourself that you will not allow anything steal your eternity in Heaven

• You need your faith in life to defeat death

• Faith gives full assurance of our salvation

• If we think that the love of God must be earned, we are wrong we do not receive the love from our great deeds, talents, and good intentions, but from the fact of its existence

• TO DEFEAT THE FEAR OF DEATH, it is necessary to know that you are loved by God and not live expecting that someday God will love you

• Sin is a conscious decision not to deny yourself pleasure

• Salvation is not something you earn

• A person becomes righteous not because he fell, passing through some tests, but because he was able to rise

• Eternity does not depend on persons or your good deeds; it depends on the relationship that you have built with the Lord

TEST
«WHERE WILL I SPEND ETERNITY»

In each statement or question of the test, there should be only one answer. Next to each answer, in brackets, is a score. Your result of the test corresponds to the obtained amount of points.

1. Do you admit the idea that you are not worthy of eternity in Heaven?
   a) I admit (1)
   b) In general, I doubt the idea (0)
   c) No, I don't admit (2)
   d) I am confident I will spend my eternity in Heaven (3)

2. Your life in eternity is based on...
   a) Assumptions (1)
   b) Guesses (0)
   c) Confidence (2)
   d) Faith (3)

3. How is salvation acquired?
   a) Special deeds of a person (1)
   b) By the presence of the cross or other Christian paraphernalia in the house (0)
   c) In prayer, repentance (2)
   d) Through faith in Jesus Christ (3)

4. If you have committed a sin, what are your next steps?

    a) I am not worried about it (0)

    b) I am ashamed (1)

    c) I am concerned about my actions (2)

    d) I ask God for forgiveness and continue to live for Him (3)

5. Who will get eternity in Heaven?

a) The person who serves others (1)

b) The person who is faithful (0)

c) The person who serves God (2)

d) The person who knows God personally as his friend (3)

RESULTS
OF THE TEST

Less than 5 points. Unfortunately, you do not think about what will happen after your death and where you will spend eternity. All your ideas are based on rituals and traditions. You believe the insignificant words of people and keep these words deep in your heart. All you need - is to stop living with the ideas from people and religious rituals. I am sure this book will bring transformation to you after reading it, and you will begin to see that God is very close to you.

6-10 points. You often think about how you need God. However, your idea is abstract, as if you look at the blurred picture and do not see a clear image. You know eternity can be close, and it depends on how close you are to God in a simple heart conversation. Read the book and imagine a future only in Heaven.

11-15 points. Death does not frighten you. You have a good foundation and you do not build only on external attributes or deeds, but on your knowledge of Jesus Christ, through which you build your eternity on a personal relationship with Him. Try always to be guided in life not by what you are doing, but only by a sincere relationship with God.

PRACTICAL TASKS

1. On what acquisition of eternity level are you? Where do you need to climb to a new level of relationship with God?

2. What is the difference between the chosen people and the called people? Explain it on your example.

3. What will you do if you have sinned? What is your plan to the satisfaction of sin?

4. What does your belief presuppose about life after death?

Recommended reading: UNIVERSITY OF LIFE - «The power of personal integrity» book. When a person is satisfied with a little, gaining something far greater, he begins to appreciate it.

Chapter 3

THE BODY IS
OUR LIMITATION

Chapter 3
THE BODY IS
OUR LIMITATION

Yesterday I drop by to have a filling in my tooth
And laughter took me over on my way:
All my life I am taking care of my future corpse
And zealously try to preserve it

Igor Guberman,
(Soviet and Israeli writer)

Each one of us have a body and that is an obvious fact. It is also a fact that our life is limited by this very body. When you feel pain, what do you care mostly about in that moment? Is it possible not to respond to pain? For example, to an aching tooth, we may say: «Come on, it will pass» Of course not, you will still find a remedy to the pain. Physical pain makes normal existence impossible, and finding the time to take care of it and relieve the pain, demonstrates to us that the body is a part of our life. For some, it's just a piece of the puzzle while for others it's all their life. They do not realize it's only a minor step between life and death. That is right. Dear reader, in this chapter we will consider a question. Is death gained on Earth? This is because physical pain brings the fear of death, informing us that our lifespan is ending.

In the previous chapter, we have touched on the subject of death, and have studied the advantages and found out that we do not actually die, but, it is our body that dies instead. What we learn is that our body is the vessel housing our soul and that the body limits our life on Earth. In addition, how do you like the following option: you have a life, you have a body, but there is no pain, no disappointment or aging? Then let us talk further on about WHAT WAITS FOR US AFTER DEATH.

THE BODY EQUALS INFIRMITIES

Joke
- Doctor, will I make money if I donate my body to science after my death?

- Of course.

- Can I donate other bodies? I can get a couple of those!

The Body – is our limit, it is something that only bears our life. Moreover, though it is our body, it in so many ways work against us, yet we devote most of our time to it. For example, if our body is sick and weak, we become less productive, out of spirit and energy. We fall behind on everything and have to catch up, we become anxious and complain about our destiny. Quite simply, we are mostly focused on our body because we put the fear of death above

life itself. Simply, if we knew and considered that it is the body that limits our life, we would OVERCOME THE FEAR OF DEATH and expect a full life in eternity. We don't see life after death, that's why when the body has the slightest injury, instead of taking it as a hint that not everything is eternal and that we should look up to Heaven, we have all sorts of procedures on our body just to gain some more time. Take this moment and change yourself and your life, but not "fix" your body and go on worshiping it. But most of the time we think not about eternity but about the body.

Summary. The fear of death is so great that solely the body influences life itself. This is a mistake, which may lead many to Hell because they have focused on themselves and their body, and do not love the Lord.

It works like that joke: «if you need bodies, doctor, so much it is not a problem, particularly because it can bring in money.» It is funny, but is worth looking into.

Here is a story of Colton Burpo, a four-year-old boy and his trip to Heaven.

He was between life and death, an emergency surgery was performed on him to save his life and the success of which even doctors were not sure. But the boy survived and told an astounding story of his trip to Heaven.

His impressions of this place were similar to other eyewitness stories: the streets of gold, many shades of color.

The boy saw Jesus and was sitting on his lap. But, what is most amazing, Colton was able to prove the truth of what he saw. He stated that he had met his sister in Heaven, who looked very much like him. She started hugging her brother, saying she was delighted to meet a member of her family and that she misses her parents. When the boy asked her name, she said that she did not have time to receive it. As it turned out, a year before the birth of the boy his mother had a miscarriage, and his sister really could have been born. However, Colton did not know about it. Besides, the boy met his great-grandfather in Heaven who died thirty years before his birth. After that meeting, the grandson recognized his grandfather from a photo, where he was portrayed in his youth.

According to the boy's story, the inhabitants of paradise did not age and lived there always young. (8)

Let us conclude this story and try to paint a picture of Heaven. A beautiful place, where all the streets are lined with gold, not the usual potholes on the road, this implies that the question of money or wealth in Heaven is not a question at all because there is an abundance of everything. An abundance of colors tell us that everything we see on the ground is merely a minuscule portion of what awaits us in Heaven.

We see green trees in the spring, and our eyes rejoice at the beauty, but on the second day, we no longer notice it. In addition, any flower or shrub blooms and carries its

fruits only for a certain period of time. In Heaven, every day, every minute, and second, we will admire it and love all the grandeur that we can see or experience with millions of cells of our body. The fields will not fade, the flowers will not dry, and the colors will not change because in Heaven there is no death, all that is there is life at its best, a complete manifestation.

Also worth noting is that the boy from the story above interacted with Jesus, and it tells us that we will be capable to communicate with everyone in Heaven, and even with God himself. Will it not be great to know Jesus personally? Anyone who reads the Bible knows that all instructive stories and parables told by Jesus to his disciples are all exciting. They also remain an instructive guide for us today and in this lifetime. But we all have the book of life, the Bible, and we need to understand this book on our own, delving into every word which tells us how to live for eternity.

In Heaven, we will be speaking about how we used it; how we lived and acted it, what guided us in making our decisions. Besides, proof of his stories authenticity are the memories of the boy who have seen everything that was there in Heaven and he was able to recite what he saw to his father. A meeting with his sister tells us that our close relatives and friends are waiting for us in Heaven, and the one who will become a part of Heaven will rejoice and look forward to seeing a loved one, and it will be a pity if the expectation is not met.

Summary. Never put life on Earth above life in Eternity, OVERCOME THE FEAR OF DEATH with your clear vision of life, which does not end on earth.

The body should not be an obstacle to our desire for Eternity. We must learn to live in the light of eternity, living our lives carefully and not just by the temporary pleasure. The first thing that we notice about a man is his body, and in fact, very few people look deeper within their eyes. We accept a person's judgment at its face value; appreciate what he wears, the look of his hair, and the scent of his body. It turns out that in a person we see only his body and thereby limit the notion of his individuality, without seeing his uniqueness. We do not notice the human intellect and do not celebrate its advantages, and do not take into account its abilities. To sum up, it turns out that to us when there is a body – there is a person, who is worthy of our attention. However, Heaven forbid if this person has a physical flaw because then that person will not exist for us. Think back, whether there were times when you saw a physical disability in another human and despised him as a person? Seeing flaws, we pay attention to them, showing excessive disgust. Imagine a picture of why it happened, or even see some kind of «movie» trying to guess why the person does not have for example a hand. The body is not something that can be sealed with seven seals and, therefore, protected from injuries and wounds. A body is just a vessel that is very vulnerable, and every day we run the risk of hurting it.

Think about what would happen to a man who spent his life only being pampered and lazy? Imagine the way we pay so much attention to other people's appearances, which sooner or later (as practice shows it's always sooner) will start to lose its former shape.

Joke

Gladiators rubbed their body with oil to accentuate their biceps. Only that the Lions looked at it simply from a culinary point of view.

We waste our time, resources, and money on our bodies, but someone else sees all this and thinks it's an act of fanaticism and nothing more. For instance, there are business people whom you would never assume to be millionaires just judging by their appearances. It is quite simple because the body for them is not a value and not a priority.

Summary. The body is not supposed to be valued over daily deeds and actions. What is the body good for tomorrow, if tomorrow might never come? If you do not appreciate every day of your life, no matter what fortune you have, you will not be able to live your life again.

A programming student from Costa Rica underwent surgery, during which she died, traveled to Heaven and came back. Graciela H. told her story.

I saw the doctors who were helping me. They were scared. They saw the vital signs of my body and performed CPR. Then they slowly began to leave the room. I could not understand why they were behaving like this.

It was surprisingly silent up there. I decided to get up. Only my doctor was standing in the same spot, looking at my body. I decided to come closer and stood beside him. I felt that he was saddened and his soul hurt. I remember that I touched his shoulder, and then he was gone... My body began to rise, caught by a strange force, and it felt wonderful. Going through the ceiling of the operating room, I found out that I could go anywhere.

As you understand, with each story it clearly shows us that the feelings remain the same, and we can feel everything in full after death. We can grieve and rejoice in everything that goes on around us. We experience it in our mind.

I found myself in a place where there were bright clouds, in some room or space... around it was light, very bright, it filled my body with energy and my heart with happiness.

I looked at my hands, they had the same shape as a human, but the fabric was different. This fabric looked like a gas mixed with white and silver, pearly glow all around my body.

I felt really beautiful. I had no mirror to take a look, but I knew I was beautiful. I saw that my hands and feet were covered with a simple white long robe of light... I had the voice of a teenager, which followed the tone of a childish voice. Suddenly, the light approached me, brighter than my body... That light blinded me.

Isn't it amazing to see and feel the warmth of all that may surround us in Heaven? The Light... it is not the first time we hear about it from people who have been in Heaven. This is a hint for us that everything will be filled with incredible light, very different from the sun which burns and does not allow us to enjoy it. Pay attention to the beauty that people enjoy, seeing themselves, their body in perfect condition. They are showing us, that their body is beautiful; you should admire and enjoy it, feeling that beauty.

I heard a real angelic voice: «You can't stay here.» I remember speaking with the light in his language telepathically, he also spoke telepathically. I cried because I didn't want to go back, he lifted me up... All this time I felt the peace that comes from the light, and it gave me strength. I could feel the love and energy. In this world, nothing can compare with that love and energy... I heard: «You were sent here by mistake, by someone's mistake. You have to go back... To come here, you'll have to perform a lot of acts... try to help people.»(10)

The potential of eternity is unlimited, and if our heroine could hear his voice and at the same time communicate with him telepathically, it tells us that in Heaven everything is perfect, not only the body and conscience but also the mind and its abilities. Do you have a pet? If so, surely you play and take care of it, in this case, you create a kind of one-way communication. Nevertheless, if we are talking about eternity and the abilities and advantages that exist out there, we will not just play with them, but also talk to them. What do you think about an opportunity not only to talk, and to respond, but also to hear words of encouragement or, hear a success story from the mouth of a kitten? Those are incredible opportunities of Heaven, which are impossible for humans and animals on Earth. The one who conquers death by their desire and belief in eternity will get the opportunity after the completion of his life on Earth.

When life is leaving the physical body in an instant, it immediately receives another body in Heaven that is not corruptible physically. According to the girl, she could not even understand what happened because the transition from one body to another occurred suddenly, and this process is almost impossible to measure with time.

One receives a new body at once, and a man who has just died, cannot understand what happened. One moment he is dead, another he is alive again, there is no sense of death. Everything happens at lightning speed - one life and immediately another one, without stopping. It is a type of condition when a person is asleep and was awakened by

someone and nothing changed. The body is transformed immediately into a new one, it can be compared to the way a snake sheds its old skin and thus, immediately the new is already there. It is the same as with the body: You leave your earthly body and immediately gets a new and perfect body. While making this transition from one state to another, we will see everything that is happening around us, our body and all the vanity, tears, weeping relatives, fear, and maybe someone's joy.

Therefore, do not run and do not build your life on your body, in any case, it will give you more to grieve over the years, but build up your actions the right way to acquire a life in Heaven, where you can experience your new special and wonderful body. Everything that you have today, prepare it for the eternity: for someone it might be the body, for another – talent, beautiful singing voice, or cooking abilities. Overestimate your life, until you possess it, OVERCOME THE FEAR OF DEATH by actions having eternity in mind.

«I'm leaving,» These poignant words of Gabriel Marquez wrote in December 2000 when a disease struck him. When the writer was met with the fear of death, he overestimated his life and saw how precious time on Earth is and how important it is to find the Source of life and to ask to live not for ourselves, but in order to better appreciate and create.

"If for a moment God were to forget that I'm a rag doll and granted me a piece of life I probably wouldn't say everything that I thought; rather, I would think about everything that I say.

I would value things, not for their worth, but for what they mean. I would sleep less, dream more, understand that for each minute we close our eyes, we lose sixty seconds of light.

I would walk when others hold back, I would wake when others sleep, and I would listen when others talk.

And, how I would enjoy a good chocolate ice cream!

If God were to give me a piece of life, I would dress simply, throw myself face first into the sun, and bring not only my body but also my soul.

My God, if I had a heart, I would write my hate on the ice, and wait for the sun to show. Over the stars, I would paint with a Van Gogh dream a Benedetti poem, and a Serrat song would be the serenade I would offer to the moon.

I would water roses with my tears, to feel the pain of their thorns and the red kiss of their petals... My God, if I had a piece of life... I would not let a single day pass without telling the people I love that I love them.

I would convince each woman and each man that they are my favorites, and I would live in love with love.

I would show men how very wrong they are to think that they cease to be in love when they grow old, not knowing that they grow old when they cease to be in love!

To a child, I shall give wings, but I shall let him learn to fly on his own. I would teach the old that death does not come with old age, but with forgetting.

So this is what I have learned from you, oh men… I have learned that everyone wants to live at the top of the mountain, without knowing that real happiness is in how it is scaled.

I have learned that when a newborn child first squeezes his father's finger in his tiny fist, he has him trapped forever.

I have learned that a man has the right to look down on another only when he has to help the other get to his feet.

From you, I have learned so many things, but in truth they won't be of much use, for when I keep them within this suitcase, unhappily shall I be dying."(11)

Do not only have thoughts of good deeds or plan to; start it today. Remember that to live for eternity is to love people, not just those you know personally, but also those

who you do not know. To love God not because you have to, but because your heart is overflowing with gratitude to Him for giving you life.

Summary. Live today as if tomorrow will never come. Tomorrow is what may or may not be, but you have today, and that is a fact. It does not matter how old you are, it is important what you did today to those around you.

OUR BODY HAS ONLY A TEMPORARY ADVANTAGE

A disease or any weakness of the body may limit it on Earth. And you do not have to look far to prove it. For example, girls and women regularly have a monthly flow. And, as a rule, it is connected with physical discomfort: this could be stomach or lower backache, chest pain and headache. This limits a women's life, at least for three days. During these three days, the woman continues to live in the usual way, because you cannot get a sick-leave for these days, but the productivity is reduced by at least 25%. Still think that the body does not limit you? Then let's talk about men and their diseases.

Emma came to work with a bad mood again. The reason for this was the sudden indisposition of her husband. Speaking of a loved one, she mentioned not once how good he is, doing everything on time, he conducts business

well, keeps the house, and takes care of it. One word, he is not a man, but a rare one. However, this is what happened the other day, when she came home from work. Emma saw Denny lying in bed, he was «unwell». Well, sick means sick, Emma thought. She offered to help in the hope that her husband doesn't need it, but as it turned out, her husband was very needy. She brought, cooked chicken soup, straightened the pillow, and rubbed his legs. The thermometer is available in her house at all times. So, throughout the evening and half of the night, Denny's temperature rose to a fatal grade, but he lay on his deathbed, capricious and demanding too much attention. The fight started with her husband's words, «Let's call the doctor, maybe you're taking care of me in a wrong way. "Then Emma made a scene, and eventually went to sleep in another room, locking the door. In the morning, she woke up and went to work. Denny slept like a baby on his favorite sofa near the TV.

If anyone recognized himself in the story, then answer. Does disease limit your body, and those who live with you? Here is a poem about a husband who is sick. Unfortunately, the author of this masterpiece is unknown.

My husband has thirty-seven and two.

With a face haggard and gray,

On white crumpled sheets,

As the victim of a frenzied cholera

Lies knees to the wall.

Lingering groan, as in childbirth,

Shaking a thermometer in his hands.

All the sorrow of the Jewish people

Stuck in the constriction of the pupil.

In strong-willed chin

Flowing foamy saliva.

He whispers pitifully and timidly:

«How are you with the children alone now?»

The apartment has ceased talking,

Nightlight illuminates barely.

Dark... omitted all the curtains...

My husband was thirty-seven and two.

✳ ✳ ✳

Men sometimes get sick in a way that their wives do not know where to go or what to do. But there are stories, in which an overlooked disease is exacerbated. For example, one woman ignored the pain in her breast, thinking that this is due to menopause. When her children literally forced her to get a checkup, it turned out that she had breast cancer in the last stage. It was treated the best way they could, but the woman died as the cancer has metastasized to distant organs. Her death could have been prevented if the patient had not neglected the symptoms and alarm bells in her life.

Summary. If something hurts, it is necessary to ask for help and not ignore the warning signs and impending death. After all, who knows whether you will have time to bring your life to eternity if you ignore your health?

If we do not overcome the fear of death, and we try to just hold on to life, doing nothing for eternity, we cannot become citizens of Heaven. In order to get the opportunity to enjoy all the benefits of living in paradise, we must not live according to the principles that dictate our body, but by the Holy Scriptures, living by its truth, and not according to the flesh.

Living by the Truth is:

Striving every day to listen to our conscience and living by the truth. Do not only play the role of a good man, but be so in thoughts and actions.

Do not steal other people's time or property even when you see that something "lies handy", get the owner's attention and be honest. Do not steal ideas; do not steal the good name of a person trying to blacken his name because of envy.

Be grateful to God for life, to your parents, and to those who helped you even with a single word in your life path.

Imagine when we think that we are dying and so afraid of death, thinking that this is the end; it really is just the beginning of the most important meetings with the one who created the history of the world. It is as if you were invited to a celebration, which brought together the most influential people of the world, your loved ones, and family, and you refused to go because you are afraid. So you change your mind and decide to go. You are greeted as a dearest guest, and all around you, there is dancing and singing, because you have come to the celebration of life, where you have gathered around you; the most precious people. Imagine the faces of those who are waiting for you in Heaven maybe it's your parents, relatives, or people you read about in the history books, but never seen. Nevertheless, they are waiting to tell you that you are dear to them. Such meetings await all new arrivals in Heaven. Jesus will welcome those who by faith and by their life served people, passing the essence of Christ's crucifixion to them that all may have salvation. And spend eternity in Heaven.

Do not trade the beauty of eternity for illusionary events, because what awaits us in Heaven, is far greater than anything we can compare with the possibilities of life on Earth. For example, you love the smell of flowers and admire the beauty of nature. However, all this is just an example of what might be waiting for you in Heaven. Flowers bloom, and then wither, they all have a certain color, and sellers in the markets try to make them even more vivid by painting them, and I do not want to mention the scent; most of them have no smell at all as they are grown artificially. In

Heaven, these flowers are blooming, and always have an incredible smell, each flower carries its individuality and anyone who inhales the smell can feel it with their whole body, with every cell of their being. These flowers do not fade, they always have an incredible color, while it can also display the color that you want to see. Today it can be a purplish-pink flower, it can be turquoise tomorrow. It all depends on your desire. We often think of how beautiful flowers on Earth are, not having any idea of what real beauty is. Still, no desire to open your life to Heaven? Then let us go further.

We live and think of how good it is to have technology. It brings new opportunities, innovation, and development. However, the human mind is still limited. All of you probably have heard that a human being uses only a small part of the mental faculties, something around 10%, but that is not the point. No matter what we have on Earth, it is important that it is a small hint for us about how we will live in Heaven.

For example, when the car was first created and now we see it every day, expensive or cheap, old or new, it does not matter. We must understand that God allowed this to be invented, to show how cool it is to own a car. Nevertheless, in Heaven, it will not only be just a car but high-speed machines that fly through the air, in another way, there exist technologies that we can only see in science fiction films. Moreover, you as a citizen of Heaven will have such a vehicle not for self-affirmation, but in order to be

able to spend time wherever you want. So do you still think you have a bed of roses on Earth?

Yes, it is good to live in a physical form on Earth, but not enough to exchange worshiping Heaven for worshiping the body. Everything should be in balance when we are taking care of our body to exist and to live for those who do not know and have not heard about the joys and benefits of Heaven. Death is an illusion that we are terrified of, and which is associated only with the death of the body, but not our spirit. Therefore, whether we like it or not, DEATH IS AN ADVANTAGE because after the death of the body we will not limit our lives with disappointment or sickness.

Let us talk about diseases: what happens to them after our physical body dies. I have three insights for you, two of which are good.

First. Our body after death will be perfect. We will make the transition from one body to another, a perfect one. We have talked about this a little bit: your body will be the same as in the best years of our youth; beautiful, resilient, flawless, and without any loose skin or injury. The body will be as perfect as we have ever seen, perfect even in the smallest ways.

Second. In Heaven, there are no diseases. Not a single disease in Heaven, there is nothing that could injure your body, mind, cells NOTHING! Everything in Heaven is the perfection of the body and minds abilities, the immensity

of ideas and the implementation of incredible desires. We will not worry about any pain, we will be complete, with one hundred percent health, and even thoughts of diseases will not arise. No time or space will harm the body, which we will gain in Heaven; it will always be in the best condition.

The third news is that not everyone will get a new body. Those who accept Christ into their hearts will get the opportunity to go to Heaven, but those who do not reconcile with God after death will see a different picture of reality, Hell.

Therefore, dear friend, we always have a choice to OVERCOME THE FEAR OF DEATH, or continue to live with it. Never bet on your body, sooner or later, it will fail. Very quickly, our physical shell wears out, gets sick, and suffers.

Summary. All we need today is to live in order to serve with our body. Hands and legs are given to us to help someone else, the eyes to notice the needs and pain of others, and a mouth to speak good words to everyone. Our whole body is given to us to add value to people, do not waste time worshiping it, but use it to help others.

A friend came out of the bathroom. She stood in front of the mirror. Eye cream, face cream, body lotion, hand lotion, foot cream, emollient lotion to elbow and heels. Well, that is it! Enough! And, I have a question: what is the point in taking a shower when you make yourself all dirty again?

Author unknown

Summary. Do not allow the body to occupy all your thoughts, and do not let disease make you focus on the body. Disease is a signal for each one of us that soon this body will become frail, as it approaches the time of our death. Disease is also a bell that gives us a reason to think about death and eternity, and today you'll have to choose where you will spend your eternity.

THE BODY WILL EVENTUALLY LET YOU DOWN

Loren saw a sharp blinding light. She could not understand what was happening around her until her eyes adjusted to the bright shine. She could not remember what was before because she was still adapting to what was happening. Therefore, she thought of work, the road, the shops, bread, and the road home. Now when she adjusted to the bright rays it all seemed different. Loren began to examine herself, her skin had a beautiful color, her body had a delightful view, and for a moment, she thought she was a young girl of twenty, not a woman, «in her fifties». Her body was so

beautiful that she was embarrassed by the fact that she admired it for so long.

There is a delightful sight of the body. In every story, we can see how people who have experienced death and saw themselves beyond this Earthly life were surprised by the look of their own body. After all, usually, when we look in the mirror, you are not always pleased with what you see, and why is everyone who has been in Heaven saying the same thing that his or her body looked so perfect that it was impossible to look away from it? In Heaven, everything is perfect, on Earth, we distort the world around us with our desires and live primarily for ourselves. In Heaven, everything has the highest form of perfection and quality, so it is not surprising that there are people who have visited it and do not like to go back to live on Earth, to which we all currently hold so dear.

Looking away from the body, Loren saw that the room was very similar to the operating room. On the table laid someone's worn out body, old, and repulsive... «Hmm - thought Loren, how old is this body, and why am I looking at it when it's such a horrible sight.» Coming closer, she began to see the hands, feet, and finally the face, and then she saw something very familiar in it. She was shocked: it was her body; she looked at herself from the outside! She was taken-aback with all the weakness of her once beloved body. It was like seeing a pair of old worn-out clothes, which long ago should have been discarded. So Loren thought, looking at herself with rejection.

To see the body as a disadvantage, even while experiencing a feeling of aversion to what previously brought pleasure is the view from the outside! I think we greatly exaggerate that small feeling of pleasure, which we have on Earth. We think we have the best of everything, but, as the proof of life after death shows; the best is waiting for us only in Heaven. On Earth, we have the semblance of a copy, a small reproduction of real life and we enjoy this, thinking that it is the limit of our dreams. Yes, this is the limit for those who do not know what awaits us after death.

Loren, a university professor, always looked after herself and her appearance, suddenly seeing all the weakness of her own body. Moreover, she could not believe that the body in which she found herself in was perfect, absolutely flawless – pure perfection. Then she had the other picture, where she saw her daughter and her husband embracing, they cried and begged the doctors to do everything possible during the operation. She realized that something happened and they worry for her and hope for a recovery. After a while, she remembered she wanted to return to her worn-out body less and less and experience the pain of rehabilitation of body and soul.

Now Loren shares her memories very rarely so that the others do not take her story as the unbelievable one. She regained consciousness, and she was told that there was an accident in which she suffered and spent a certain time in a coma, underwent a series of operations, and is now recovering from the shock. The only thing that makes

Loren so childishly happy is the moment when she saw the opportunity to live a full life without barriers, both in her body and in her mind.

The body is a disappointment. It will disappoint us, and it will happen sooner than later. Talking to people, I noticed the same trend, especially among women, no matter what age they are, they are always dissatisfied with their bodies. Communicating with teenagers, I hear the same problems, communicating with adult women, I see their discontent. All of them have one argument: the body, which they have, does not satisfy them. It is simple: if a woman is focused on the body, it will always disappoint her, too thin or too thick, too tall or too short. Moreover, any temporary defect may bring a woman into hysteria. If women were in a body that pleased, delighted, and gave them a sense of youth and absolute health – issues related to appearance are not noticed then some may not feel so badly like they do. But in order to obtain such a perfect body, you do not need to live on Earth. The body is a trigger causing the fear of death, but to OVERCOME THE FEAR OF DEATH one must not live for the body, but for eternity. Death is an advantage, whether we agree with it or not.

Summary. If we learn to see the positive aspects and advantages, we will automatically cease to be afraid of what we would look like. There are two new insights:

First, In Heaven, our bodies will be perfect. It will not cause the slightest displeasure, but only joy and admiration,

because every cell of it would be filled with love and perfection. Life begins when we die. Our minds will not look for what is wrong with us. We will see beauty everywhere, and the perfection of the body will not go unnoticed. No need to use creams, makeup, and other «disguises» for the body because everything will be perfect, beautiful and natural.

Second, is that not everyone will get an opportunity to acquire such a perfect body. Those who pay more attention to their physical form on Earth will not be able to acquire a perfect body in eternity. Such a person is not able to serve his body to people or God. The life of such people is limited by their own desires and concerns.

Unfortunately, the one, who lives only for himself, spends years of his life to ensure his needs are met, does nothing in order to get to Heaven. You can argue that there is nothing wrong with that but on the other hand, there is nothing good in it too. This is the answer: «I know your deeds, that you are neither cold nor hot. I wish you were either one or the other! So, because you are lukewarm- neither hot nor cold - I am about to spit you out of my mouth. «(Bible, Revelation 3: 15-16). When a person is cold, he knows that his salvation is hidden in reconciliation with God; he is the one who heard and never accepted the sacrifice of Jesus Christ. A Hot person is the one who knew and accepted Jesus as his Lord and Savior, who understands the importance of a relationship with God, walks with God and serves people.

The warm person is the one who accepted Jesus as Lord and Savior but is being carried away by self; this person Lives for self, and will be rejected by God. He won't be invited to the throne of the Heavenly Father in Heaven.

So do not count on the body, in any case, it is temporary, begin to build a life on Earth, so that after death, to hear you are worthy to enter the house of the Father. All the same, your body is going to disappoint you, whether you are 15 or 45 years of age there is no difference, on the Earth the body is not perfect.

DIE TO LIVE

The body is a shame. So it is incorporated into the stereotypes of the society that children should be ashamed of their bodies, adolescents are disappointed in it, and the adults blame it. There is no reason to be ashamed of the body or feel humiliated, but as a rule, all complexes are based precisely on imaginary physical appearance.

Many women build their whole life only worshiping their body, and then they themselves suffer from it. For example, prostitution is the sale of one's body and leading an ungodly lifestyle. The woman considers herself unworthy, shameful, humiliated, and inferior. The body builds a dysmorphic disorder, held hostage to its scope and limitations. Therefore, when it is weak, it is increasing the fear of death. And it binds and limits life and all thoughts are not of the advantages of death, on the contrary, all

thoughts are aimed at how the Earth will live without us as it will outlive relatives, children. While the most important thing about it is worth considering what will happen to you, what will you occupy in eternity after the end of your Earthly life?

Here we present you the memories of Polish artist Alicja Zientek, who experienced clinical death.

My clinical death occurred during pregnancy. January 8, 1989. Around 10:00 p.m., I started bleeding. There was no pain, only severe weakness, and chills. I realized that I was dying.

The doctors were connecting different devices, and the anesthesiologist began to read aloud their testimony. Soon I began to choke and heard the words of the doctor: I am losing contact with the patient, I cannot feel her pulse but it is necessary to save the child. Voices began to subside around, their faces blurred, and then there was darkness. Again…

I found myself in the operating room. However, now I felt well, easy. Doctors bustled around the body lying on the table. I approached him. I laid there. There, on the table, I lay like a lifeless deck, and at the same time, I was here healthy and full of energy.

And, even able to float in the air. Miraculous healing? But, why can no one see me?

The inner state of people who have seen the beauty of Heaven is striking after each story. The body becomes light, full of strength and energy, there is no pain and weakness, and there is a sense of healing. In eternity, there is no healing, disease, weakness in the body, emotional instability, or psychological disorders. That is what it means to live without thinking about how to run to the drugstore and buy another painkiller at the slightest pain in the body.

I was sure that I was alive because I had sight, smell, and touch. I just did not feel the weight of my body. Because of the unusual condition, I was seized by a strong fear. I realized that if no one can see me or hear me, it means that I became different.

From the ceiling came a shining white light. It landed on me not blinding me or burning me. I realized that the beam is calling to him, promising relief from isolation. Without thinking, I went to meet him.

I moved along the line, though invisible to the top of the mountain, feeling completely safe.

The release of the body from prison that is what happened to our heroine. She was beckoned by Heaven. The story featured a woman, and that familiar bright light that could give confidence and security on the level of inner conviction. No need waiting to calm down, waiting to be supported by a word, or ensure we are secured when we are wounded or feel fear. In Heaven, everything happens

by itself, as love and life are vital and essential components of it.

Reaching the top, I saw a wonderful country, a harmony of bright and at the same time, almost transparent colors, sparkling around. It is impossible to describe in words. I was all eyes looked around, and all that is around filled me with such a delight that I cried, my God, what a beauty! I have to write all of this. I was seized with a burning desire to return to my old reality and describe all that I saw here. Thinking about this, I again found myself in the operating room. But, this time, looking at it as if from the outside, as if from cinema screen. And, the film seemed black and white. The contrast with the colorful scenery, the wonderful country was calling, and I decided to move there again.

Everything described in this episode indicates that people will be extraordinary in Heaven. The possibility of movement, will not be on the ground realm rather at the level of thoughts and desires. Want to go to Australia, no problem. You want to see the Great Wall of China, it is possible by a simple effort of thought. Is it not wonderful to have such mind power? We only dream of it on Earth. Heaven is beautiful, it is filled with inexhaustible colors of life that are not available during our Earthly life. What will happen after death? I do not know for anyone, but for myself, I am waiting to live in the beauty of Heaven and enjoy all other possibilities in Heaven.

Even our heroine herself notes how striking the contrast between the Heavenly beauty and what happened to her in the operating room: a black and white reality of life on Earth is opposed to her story of a very colorful Heaven.

A sense of glamor and excitement did not pass. And, in my head every now and then the question arose: «Was I alive or not?» Moreover, I was afraid that if I go too far into this unknown world, I would not return. In addition, at the same time, I did not want to part with such a miracle. However, the desire to quickly capture on canvas and show other people this amazing land emerged with renewed vigor. At this point, something stopped me (as if grabbing the back of my neck) and pushed through the transparent bluish barrier

Now I was not looking at the beauty of this paradise, I was in it! Staring at everything.

I moved on. All around, was a sea of red tulips. I leaned over and began to admire one. Amazingly, we could mentally communicate with each other! And, he was telling me about himself. I stayed with the other flowers, and they talked to me. Everyone had his or her wishes and concerns like here on Earth. Suddenly, I was horrified that I am stepping on living creatures. I looked at the ground. But, it turned out that I do not cause any harm to the flowers, so easy was my pace. And, I realized: everything is constructed as follows. That all the creatures of nature are equally important and have the same value. As if in reward for my understanding,

a gorgeous white dress suddenly appeared, and in my mind it was made: "Now you can choose a path that will go on."

I was again seized by the desire to share what people experienced here; joyful feelings they experienced; I decided to go back to them. With great regret, I soared over the edge of the miraculous. In flight, I turned back again and again to enjoy the magnificent spectacle.

So I went through a near-death experience and being away from the body. Now I know that those who have gone through something like this, are not mentally ill, but normal people. Do not stand out from the rest, they came back from «over there», knowing these feelings and experiences that do not fit the conventional concepts and ideas. And, I know that during that tour I acquired more knowledge. I could also comprehend, and understand more than in all my previous life. (12)

Do not wait for the day your die, to be able to get to eternity, you need to live each day putting Heaven as your highest value. Never compare life on Earth to life in Heaven, it is like trying to compare life on the planet Earth and the impossibility of living on the planet Mars. All that we hold on Earth, we are afraid to lose just because we can see it and we have it today; but Heaven is what we have to revive in our lives, overcome the fear of DEATH by gaining life.

There are two more insights:

First. No matter how you lived before, there is no partiality with God when he takes one and rejects others. No. The one who has repented of his sins has the opportunity to live forever in Heaven.

There is a story in the Bible (John 8: 3-11). One day Jesus taught in the temple of Jerusalem. The teachers of the law and the Pharisees brought in a woman caught in adultery. They made her stand before the group and said to Jesus, "Teacher, this woman was caught in the act of adultery. In the Law, Moses commanded us to stone such women. Now, what do you say?"

They were using this question as a trap, in order to have a basis for accusing him.

But, Jesus bent down and started to write on the ground with his finger. When they kept on questioning him, he straightened up and said to them, "Let anyone of you who is without sin be the first to throw a stone at her." Again, he stooped down and wrote on the ground.

At this, those who heard began to go away one at a time, the older ones first, until only Jesus was left, with the woman still standing there. Jesus straightened up and asked her, "Woman, where are they? Has no one condemned you?"

"No one, sir," she said.

"Then neither do I condemn you," Jesus declared. "Go now and leave your life of sin."

As we can see, Jesus did not condemn the woman, but put forward one condition: she should not sin again. Therefore, analyzing the past, do not feel sorry for what you have done, or self-pity. The goal of each person is to prevent the repetition of past mistakes. Therefore, if you are afraid to die a sinner, accept the Lord into your heart and do not let sin affect your life.

The second news is that not everyone will go to Heaven and see the real life because they forgive themselves. Self-deprecation does not give one the opportunity to acquire freedom and faith in the fact that on the cross, Jesus took all your disgrace and shame, everything that we come through on our way to repentance. We condemn ourselves out of ignorance, and the reason is an unwillingness to live a completely different life. We do not forgive ourselves, so as not to change and to be able to continue to feel sorry for our misdeeds. Not forgiving ourselves today, we will never be able to understand and take advantage of living in Heaven because we consider ourselves unworthy of such an award.

Do not waste your resources on begging for forgiveness, God desires you amend your relationship with Him, repent sincerely in your heart, confess Him into your life and begin to live so as not to repeat the mistakes of the

past, freeing yourself from the fear of death by faith in your salvation. The goal of every person should be to discover an opportunity to enjoy the purity of the body and mind, and after a life of holiness on Earth, to enter Heaven a place where we will know the true purity of our body.

RELEASE FROM THE PRISON OF THE BODY

The Parable about the tourist

One American tourist visited a famous sage.

The tourist was surprised to discover that the sages home consists of only one room filled with books, tables and benches that was all.

- Rabbi, where is your furniture? - Asked the American with surprise.

- Where's yours? - Asked the sage.

- Mine? But, here I am passing through. I am a tourist here.

- Me too.

For a good comparison! We are all tourists to this land. I would say that we are migrant workers populating the Earth, and also with the desire to get rich but do not understand the true purpose of staying here, unfortunately, we lose the «ticket» to Heaven. And, at the end of life, it becomes clear that there was a chance, but in our ignorance or pride, it was not used.

Not to be left with anything, and not to regret years spent on meaningless adventure, close your eyes now and try to imagine a picture of how you would like to live. Draw all that you dream about: in which city would you have settled on which continent, whatever house you have, what ideas you have implemented, what kind of friends? Now imagine how much money you need to accomplish it on Earth. Understand that you can get all these in Heaven, where you never get bored, life is overflowing and, you can have all the things dreamed about during your Earthly life. All these will be available in Heaven, and completely free. But this will be possible on one condition: if you do not follow personal desires, but the truth of life, realizing that sin is what stands between you and your victory over the fear of death. Abandoning sin, you will win and gain the freedom from the fear of death because the belief in Eternity will be your relieve.

Earlier in this chapter, we looked at the body as a limiter in our Earthly life, and at the same time as one without which we could not exist on Earth. And if we neglect our bodies, treat them irresponsibly, we thus

are bringing about a sooner end to it. Moreover, in fact, it is not always good. For example, if you destroy your body with drugs or prostitution, you are increasing the chances of dying suddenly, without any «warnings» from sickness or disease. Destroying your body, you speed up the approach of death, and without taking the possibility of salvation in Jesus and having a true understanding of your stay on Earth, this is a straight road to Hell.

We have a body, and that's a fact, but it is given to us not to worship it but to serve people. You go to work, not only to dress up and show how good you look, but also to engage in productive activities. To take responsibility, and to generate new ideas. As people like to say, we have a head not only for a hairstyle but also to think.

The fear of death affects people who do not recognize God in their lives, refusing to believe that life continues after death and relying on chance. But, at the same time afraid of death, because in their head as they think about everything, they do not find answers of what will follow.

Without specifying a path for the future today, you will not understand what awaits you after death. We admire examples of famous historical characters, episodes of their lives, great deeds, but do not always know their position in relation to the end of their lives. One group of researchers conducted a study of famous atheists before their death, such as Friedrich Nietzsche and Marilyn Monroe, Lenin and Voltaire, and they also analyzed a joke from the engineer

who built the 0Titanic», and also what a certain pop idol, John Lennon said before death... The results were incredible.

Friedrich Nietzsche. Philosopher. Became insane, and was locked up in an asylum for the rest of his life.

Voltaire. Great quizzes of God. He had a horrible end. He screamed all night, begging for mercy. His nurse later admitted: «For all the money in Europe, I did not want to see such a death that Voltaire had, the death of an unbeliever."

David Hume. Atheist. Before his death, he was constantly shouting: «I am in flames!» His despair was terrible.

Napoleon. Emperor: His doctor wrote: «The emperor died alone, abandoned by all. His death-struggle was terrible".

Charles IX. The King of France. «I was lost. I understand that clearly.»

Hobbes. English philosopher. «I'm standing in front of a terrible leap into the darkness.»

Lenin. «The leader of the world revolution.» He died, in insanity. Asked the table and chairs for the forgiveness of his sins. How strange was that for a man who was the leader of millions of people.

Genrikh Yagoda. One of the main leaders of the Soviet State Security Organization (the Cheka, GPU, OGPU, NKVD). «There must be a God. He is punishing me for my sins».

Grigory Zinoviev. Comrades of Lenin, who was shot on Stalin's orders. «Hear, O Israel, the Lord our God is one God» is the last words of one of the leaders of the atheist state.

Winston Churchill. British Prime Minister during World War II. «What a fool I am!»

Yaroslavsky. President of the international atheist movement. «Please burn all my books. Look at the Saint! He's been waiting for me for a long time. He's here!»

John Lennon. One of the founders and member of the group, The Beatles. Being at the peak of popularity (1966), during an interview for a leading US magazine, he said: «Christianity will end, it will disappear. I do not have to argue about that. I am certain. Jesus was OK, but his subjects were too simple, today we are more famous than Him! «Shortly after, Lennon was tragically killed. One psychopath shot him at close range six times. It is noteworthy that the killer did it in order to get his popularity and fame throughout the world as the murderer of the famous singer.

Tancredo Neves De Almeida. Brazilian politician. During the Presidential campaign, he said if he got 500,000

votes from his party, not even God would remove him from Presidency. Sure, he got the votes, but he got sick a day before being made President, then he died.

Engineer, who built "Titanic". After the construction of Titanic, a reporter asked him how safe the Titanic would be. With an ironic tone, he said: "Not even God can sink it", the result: I think you all know what happened to the Titanic.

Marilyn Monroe. Famous actress. She was visited by Billy Graham during the presentation of a show. He said the Spirit of God had sent him to reach out to her. After hearing, what the Preacher had to say, she said: 'I don't need your Jesus'. A week later, she was found dead in her apartment.

In 2005 in Campinas, Brazil a group of friends, drunk, went to pick up a friend. A mother accompanied her to the car and was so worried about the drunkenness of her friends and she said to the daughter holding her hand, who was already seated in the car: 'My Daughter, Go With God and, May He Protect You. She responded: 'Only If He (God) travels in the trunk, cause inside here it's already full'. Hours later, news came by that they had been involved in a fatal accident, everyone had died, it was impossible to recognize what car it was, but surprisingly, the trunk was intact. The police said there was no way the trunk could have remained intact. To their surprise, inside the trunk was a crate of eggs, none was broken. (13)

Summary. Each of us now has a choice to live the way we want, corrupting and destroying the body, or accepting Jesus as our Lord and Savior, and OVERCOMING FEAR OF DEATH, to live fully.

For those who live not only for themselves, there is good news: DEATH FOR YOU WILL BE AN ACQUISITION. Fear will not be able to take hold of you because you are sure that everything that you have is sent to serve Heaven, God, and people. There is no fear when you know how beautiful life is in Heaven.

The soul at death leaves the physical body, which is worn out and we acquire a new, incorruptible body. It is as if a person had been in prison for ten, twenty, or thirty years of their life, and then finally heard a surprising verdict: you are justified and now you can go free. This man who had lived all these years in confinement, walked, ate, talked, read books, and suddenly acquires the true meaning of life. He leaves his prison, his place of confinement, and gets a different possibility: now he can see the sun, the beauty of the surrounding people, to talk with different interesting people, eat what he wants, and go where he wants. Such a person becomes life itself. So our transition from one temporary residence in our body to another world after death is a way out of the prison and the failure of the pain and frustration of our body. Isn't it wonderful to realize that Earthly existence is just a prison, but what happens after death, the beginning of our real, true life?

Talking about the body, I want to give you one more argument in favor of the fact that our body is not worth all that attention it gets, as the acquisition is not for us, but, in fact, a burden. I compare it with a spacesuit for astronauts.

In order to go out into the open in space, scientists came up with a special suit. In space, certain conditions which we are used to on Earth, do not work. The same is true with us. During our life on Earth, we cannot exist without a body. The normal body is like a spacesuit, without which life is impossible in space, because the body will not stand the atmospheric pressure, this will lead to death.

Without this «second body,» it is impossible to be in space because the suit protects the human body from the external environment. The suit has a seal, it is inconvenient to deal with it at first, but with subsequent practices improvement occurs. Being without the suit makes coping impossible, as the person will have a lot of factors to overcome, especially the weightlessness there and as a result the person is prone to serious and sometimes fatal injuries.

Our Earthly, physical body is vulnerable too. We have already mentioned that it can be in pain or, it brings disappointment, sickness, and disease. Like it or not, our life on Earth depends on this «costume». Nobody – no existence on Earth, but if there is a soul, and spirit, even when the body dies, we will continue to live as someone in Heaven or someone in Hell.

To give an example of the vulnerability of the body, let us look at the vulnerability of the suit.

A dangerous incident happened during the first cosmonaut exit into space in 1965. After completing the first spacewalk program, Alexei Leonov experienced difficulties in returning to the ship, after releasing the railing, and because of the weightlessness, he couldn't get his legs into the airlock hatch of the spacecraft «Voskhod». This was due to the fact that the suit Leonov was wearing was a swollen and soft type. Having made several attempts to enter the gateway feet first, the astronaut decided to enter into it with the head first. He turned the pressure regulator, lowered the level of overpressure in the suit from 0.4 atm to 0.27 atm, which allowed him to return to the airlock. Once inside, the cosmonaut with great difficulty turned and closed the hatch. Then the airlock was inflated, the pressure therein equal to the pressure in the cabin. Cosmonaut Leonov returned to the ship. (14)

Our body is a kind of suit which helps us to exist and live on this Earth, but sooner or later we will lose it and enter into a new shell, which belongs to us. Infact, our true body is a natural acquisition, which allows us to exist with no restriction. After all, when our physical body is sick, we become strength less; we can feel great inside, but if the body hurts, it creates a sense of fear and uncertainty.

Summary. We are afraid of death because of the body, not thinking that, we will gain a lot more when we lose it.

The physical shell limits us and actually reminds us daily about what we should care about, but the priority of life should be to serve with a body and to acquire a true body after death.

Let us summarize the main results of this chapter.

1. Diseases are tips for all of us that sooner or later we will leave our body on Earth. After physical death, each of us will be able to enter into another body; a perfect body. But this opportunity is not granted to everyone. Only those who have served and lived not for the sake of solving their problems, but helped other people sincerely, humbling their hearts before God, and acknowledging His Lordship over them.

2. The body is frustrating, and it will disappoint us again and again. A person can stay in the right mind, but without the body under his control. So do not rely on the body as a value in your life, it is the temporary home of our soul. The body that you will get in Heaven will be perfect and flawless.

3. On Earth, the body is a shame for a man, but in Heaven, everything is different. In Heaven, the body becomes a decoration.

4. The body limits us on Earth and is given a limited time, so at the end of the day, we have the chance to go back to live in Heaven. We should now fight for this opportunity on Earth, to never regret it later. Self-pity for a lifetime will not lead to anything because at the end of the day it will be too late to change anything.

GOLDEN TRUTH

• Pain does not allow the body to exist normally, and if we take time out to reduce the pain in any way, then the body becomes a part of our life.

• On Earth, it is the body that limits the usefulness of our lives.

• All that is in Heaven is the perfection of both body and mind abilities, the immensity of ideas and opportunities for all of the most incredible desire.

• Never bet on your body, eventually, it will still fail you.

• All we need today is to live, serving with your body.

• After death, our new body will be perfect and will not cause the slightest discontent.

• Those who live worshiping themselves and their bodies on Earth, will not be able to get the perfect body in eternity.

• Do not count on the body, which is temporary in this life, begin to build a life on Earth by freeing self from the fear of death.

• If we do not care for the body, we will approach death faster.

• By destroying the body, we are approaching the moment of death without the possibility of repentance and a true awareness on Earth.

• The body is given to us for one purpose to serve others, to solve the problems of the society and become supporters for others.

TEST

«There was a body here,
What was left when it disappears?»

In each statement or question of the test, there should be only one answer. Next to each answer, in brackets, is a score. Your result of the test corresponds to the obtained amount of points.

1. What is your body for?
a) Beauty (1)
b) I have not thought about it (0)
c) My body is my life (1)
g) My body is my chance to be a man (2)
d) My body is given to me for service (3)

2. If your body was defective, would you...
a) Blame fate (0)
b) Think it was useless (1)
c) Accept the situation (1)
d) Try to live on (2)
d) Look for opportunities to prove yourself, even
  with disabilities (3)

3. Looking in the mirror, what do you see in it?
a) I see myself (0)
b) I can see my body (1)
c) Some disadvantages (1)
d) I can see me and my desires succeed (2)
d) I see that time is rapidly flying forward,
   bringing me closer to Heaven (3)

4. What is important to you to live today or to live in Eternity?
a) Of course, today it's what you already have (0)
b) A bird in the hand is worth two in the bush. (1)
c) I like to think about eternity, but I have
   concerns today (2)
d) All of what I am doing today brings me closer
   to eternity in Heaven (3)

5. Are you happy with a possibility of life in Heaven?
a) No, it's all in the abstract (0)
b) I do not know, I will consider it (1)
c) It would be desirable, of course, but I will
   think about it later on (1)
d) I am interested in this opportunity (2)
d) I'm excited to be able to live in Heaven (3)

RESULTS
OF THE TEST

Less than 5 points. Unfortunately, you live for yourself. Your apathy says that you are not interested in anything at all. So you live like that, from situation to situation, while not having an interest in life itself. It carries a certain danger if you do not value life, you can lose what is valuable to you. Read a book, filled with the knowledge of Heaven, dream and aspire to get your happiness in Heaven.

6-9 points. You live for the sake of the body and you pursue what you want to see. You act on your mood, or for situations that happen around you. You live the expectations of the future while doing nothing today. While reading the book, you can set goals and plan how to begin to live today to invest in the future.

10-15 points. You established priorities in your life that is why it is not hard for you to see the end of your physical existence because you did not place value on it. You set a goal to reach the maximum for Eternity, to get a life in Heaven. While reading the book, you see more clearly the way your service is taking you to, and it will increase your desire to go forward. You will know why sufferings on Earth are needed, and understand that they will lead you to life in Heaven.

PRACTICAL
TASKS

1. Is the body a significant part of your life? What have you experienced or achieved with the body you received?

2. Write down what you will gain by losing your Earthly body? In your opinion, what are the five advantages of a body in Heaven?

3. Do you live for others, are you serving them so that you can get to Heaven? Explain your answer by listing at least five arguments.

4. What are the three new things you grasped after studying this chapter?

Recommended books UNIVERSITY OF LIFE - «Overcome from fear.» Acquiring inner freedom, you will be free to think about the future. You will begin to live fully without fear of losing either their bodies or their lives.

Chapter 4

THE CAT DID IT!

Chapter 4
THE CAT DID IT!

In the previous chapter, we talked about the imperfections of our body and that life is not worth it when we consider pleasing the body as our main goal. In this case, the question arises: what is life and where are we in this life? So, **we're putting a lot of time towards what is not the essence of our existence, therefore, the body is not our whole life and life on Earth - is not forever, and everything in it is temporary, transitory, and the ability to manage it does not belong to us.** It's an illusion of life we are afraid to lose. Fear of death, we do not understand that it dissipates when we know what awaits us.

In this chapter, we will talk about what the true purpose of life on Earth is, and why we spend precious time on things that will not bring results, and also things that will not leave a trace for us to be remembered after death.

THE VALUE OF ONE DAY

We bring you the story of a man who suffered clinical death.

I had a heart attack. I suddenly found myself in a black vacuum, and I realized that I left my physical body. I knew that I was dying, and I thought, «God, I would have lived better if I knew it would happen today. Please help me».

Often we're forced to make important decisions only when something terrible happens in our lives. We are ready to promise anything and even swear not to repeat past mistakes, but as soon as the situation changes for the better, everything returns back to normal. But, when we are on the precipice of life, we only have regrets, if we do not change our attitude to life and death.

Immediately I began to get out of this darkness into something pale gray, continuing to move, slipping in this space. Then I saw a gray mist and approached it. It seemed to me that I did not move as quickly as I would like; I understood that if I approached, I could see something through it.

Behind this fog, I saw people. They looked just like people on Earth, and I have seen something that could be mistaken for some kind of buildings. Everything was permeated with an amazing light, refreshing, golden yellow, warm, and soft, not like the ones we see on Earth.

That's another clue for us that people live in Heaven, and they are just like us, look the same, each with their own body, each with their own appearance. There are buildings, and, as we have said before, people are living in Heaven, having their houses, estates. They do not just walk the streets they live as fully as possible.

The hero of our story saw a great light around him. This again testifies that during our life we cannot observe such a thing since it doesn't exist on Earth, it is present only in Heaven. This light is soft, gentle, has a golden shade. Gold attracts our gaze, it is considered valuable, precious, rare metal on Earth, but in Heaven, there is no lack of it: the roads and buildings are made with it. A lovely soft light is not only pleasing to the eye, it also brings joy and warmth. In other words, we'll feel it with our body, eyes, and ears. Since our body can be so sensual in Heaven, then we should not allow Hell at the end of our Earthly life. Because staying in Hell is associated with constant pain.

As I approached, I felt that I passed through this fog, and it was an amazing, joyful feeling. In human language, there are no words that could describe it. However, my time to move through the fog probably has not come yet. Right in front of me I saw a relative who had died many years ago. He blocked my path, saying, «Go back, your work on Earth is not finished yet. Now, go back! «I did not want to, but I had no choice, and I instantly returned to my body". Once again, I felt this terrible pain in my chest.

Let's analyze this story in order to see the benefits of Heaven and abandon the fear of death once and for all. Life after death is real, as real as what you did today. It is not that you do not wake up when it's already happened. Considering the events behind the story, we can see the same recurring details, and the most important of them: everyone who made a trip to Heaven, enjoyed this moment in their life. People who got into Heaven were happy and filled with the love of what they perceived as the body and mind.

Heaven is available to all, but it's not always possible to make a choice in its favor. This happens because we do not think about the future, we do not consider death as an opportunity and or possibility to live, we don't relate consciously to each day of our life. We think that today is just one more day, we have lived. But, neglecting one day, we can say that we neglect life as a whole, and who knows maybe this will be the last day for someone.

Summary. *For whom, a day of life is of no value, the whole of life is not of value.* Devaluing a day of our life, we only strengthen the fear of death, because unconsciously and irresponsibly we belong to eternity. Ignoring all the clues of life on Earth, we limit our chances of continuing life after death. We can overcome the fear of death when eternity becomes a daily sense of each year, day, and minute of life on Earth.

A modern parable about life

A few weeks ago, I had my breakfast: prepared some coffee, took the morning paper and sat down to listen to the radio. I turned the knob until suddenly my attention was drawn by a velvet voice of an old man. He said something about «a thousand balls.» I'm interested in, he did sound louder and leaned back in his chair.

- Well, - said the old man, - I bet that you are very busy at work. Yesterday, Today, and Tomorrow. Yes, you get paid a lot, but they buy your life for this money.

Think about it: you don't spend that time with your loved ones. I would not believe that you need to work all the time to make ends-meet. You work to satisfy your needs. But, know that this is a vicious circle and the more money, the more you want, and the more you work to get. At one point ask yourself, «Do I really need another blouse or a car.» And, for that, you're willing to miss your daughter's first dance performance or your son's sporting event? Let me tell you something that really helped me and bear in mind the most important thing in my life.

Look, one day I sat down and counted. The average person lives 75 years. I know, some live less, others longer ... But the average age of life is about 75 years. Now let's multiply 75 by 52 (the number of Sundays per year), and it turns out there is 3900 Sundays in your life. When I thought about it, I was fifty-five. This meant that I have lived for about

2900 Sundays. And, I had only 1000 left. So I went to the toy store and bought 1000 small plastic balls. I placed them all in one transparent jar.

After that, every Sunday, I pull out one ball. I noticed that when I did it and saw that the number of balls is reduced, I began to pay more attention to the true values of life. There is nothing more powerful than watching as you reduced the number of days destined for you! Now listen to the last thing I would like to share with you today before I embrace my beloved wife and go with her for a walk. This morning I pulled the last ball from my jar. So every other day is a gift for me. I accept it with gratitude and give friends and loved one's warmth and joy. You know, I think that this is the only way to live life. I regret nothing.

Do you live for real, or just live aimlessly with the time allotted to you? Are you asking yourself questions like how many «Sunday balls» are left in your life? What do you spend your time doing, and whether it will result in your life? To live each day with gratitude, giving others the joy and warmth regardless of the circumstances occurring in your life, that's what it means to cherish every moment of life. To appreciate every day as an opportunity to give ourselves so someone gains confidence in Heaven. Everyday handing themselves for others to go to Heaven «empty» without the unspoken words of love, unspoken gratitude, without unrealized ideas, without the help of which you did not provide. Go «empty» it is to sow themselves and their lives in other people.

Summary. *The one who cherishes every moment perceives the interest and importance of this life and is able to give it to others.*

THERE IS NO PERFECTION

We are often in a hurry, not knowing where we're running to. We work without seeing any sense in it, but simply to serve a nine-to-five routine, we say words to people we love, that we end up regretting; we educate our children on a routine, because "it's necessary". But, all this does not carry the enjoyment of life. It runs past us, and we simply have no time to think about our future existence. That's how our heroine Jane lived.

Jane is 57. A year ago she retired. Sitting on a bench near the house, the woman looked away, and suddenly saw something incredible. Something very tenacious held her gaze, which surprised her. Covering her face with wrinkled hands, Jane began to cry. Hair fell from under her shawl; her eyes were deep on her face. She wiped her tears and thought that for the first time in her life she saw something much more important than all her vanity cases altogether, she saw Heaven. She finally saw the beauty that she neglected for so many years. After all, what is always there usually stays unnoticed. Jane cried not because she did not notice anything, but because of life as if it never happened. More than half of her life, she simply existed, and not for someone, but just for herself, husband and children. But, where are they now...

The children have all grown up, they have their own families. They come twice a year to visit their parents. Her husband spends all his time with «friends in misfortune.» Jane choked in tears, all she owned was this life, which raced past without her participation. Heaven, the beauty of Heaven, made Jane think about what will happen tomorrow. What happens after life? Where would she end up? And, the woman was suddenly scared by the fact that in all the years of her life she had never asked herself that question.

Dear reader, have you ever asked yourself these questions? Have you paid attention to something more important than just the mundane affairs of the day? Have you thought about Heaven and eternity? Maybe you have had thoughts that you are not worthy, poorly lived your life and will never become a part of Heaven?

Summary. *It is not important that you have thoughts about these questions, it is important what you are going to do next when you finish thinking.*

Yes, we're not perfect, but do not blame yourself or think that this is necessary to come to terms with it. If you have remorse for your actions, words, and deeds are different from perfection, remember the words of Jesus: «Who is without sin among you, let him cast the first stone.» This suggests that even God himself does not expect perfection from us, but He teaches us to live differently. If you think of death as a terrifying moment of your life, start thinking of it as a mandatory condition for the acquisition

of eternal life. If you've never thought about Eternity, start to see it in your daily routine. Answering to your question, whether you live for yourself, or for merits. Don't hold yourself a prisoner to the fear of death, because it is still going to happen anyway.

To live for Eternity is:

. To live loving God and people, not to worship your body, habits, and desires.

Appreciating every day and every moment of life, knowing that this time brings you to the eternal Heaven.

To live so that there is something to share with others. All you have share with those who need it; it may be the word of faith to those who are oppressed and depressed, things from your closet that you do not wear; you can give to those who have nothing to wear, it can be a look that will give confidence to someone or a piece of bread to satisfy someone's hunger.

Whether we like it or not, our flesh is sinful, but we must always strive for perfection. For example, your child has committed a theft at the store, and you are a loving parent. Realize that this may become a habit. Promptly apologize to the store owner. Teach your child not to do it again, You're sure to punish the child, depriving him of any advantages, but you must do everything to make sure it does not happen again. So, why is it that when it comes

to a child, we try all possible ways to teach him to change, but when it comes to ourselves, we agree with our habits and way of life, comforting ourselves that it's part of our life and character, and therefore so hard to give it up.

So, when you teach a child, you do not want him to live badly, ending his life in prison, you do not want the child to become useless to the world. But when it comes to your personal life, you in fact, agree to spend eternity in Hell. Do away with habits that are not pleasing, reject every form of irresponsibility. If you agree with and like your imperfections, It becomes an excuse not to change and to live higgledy-piggledy. You do not even analyze the process of life, and it is an irresponsible attitude. But if you continue to live under the old scheme, it is already possible to say what will happen after your death; an eternity in Hell.

Leave strangers alone, do your job and spend your strength fighting your own and not someone else's imperfections.

Unknown Author

That's how life goes: we do focus on people, forgetting to make important changes in our lives. Remembering our heroine Jane, I want to note that her life was wasted, and she understood it only in her 57th year. In fact, her life wasn't hers. It's like life there but turns out that in the everyday hustle and bustle it does not belong to us.

Summary. *Life is a certain period before death, which we do not control, but the responsibility for that lies just on us.* If we live it just to satisfy our own needs, it will turn out like in the proverb: We must therefore not only think about our imperfections, but how to change ourselves in order to prepare for the exit from our physical body.

Summary. *Spend every day of your life with the realization that you do not just exist, but already live for eternity.* All that you have, including fractions of a second of your life, belongs to you.

In Heaven, there is no such thing as an imperfection or inconsistency. Everything exists with the highest standards. Everything in eternity has the highest degree of perfection. For example, we have said that our body will be perfect as we never had while living on Earth. Though that is not all. In Heaven, all the people around you will be perfect, and all thoughts and words, appearance, and actions will focus on love and respect. Moreover, roads, buildings, animals, trees, and flowers will be perfect. Everything will bring joy and inspiration. There is no such thing like shame or resentment, or disappointment in Heaven because everything is perfect.

PERISHABILITY; VISIBLE ACQUISITIONS

Joke

At night in the park:

- Life or money?

Silence.

- Life or money?

- Wait, am I thinking...

It seems to be a joke, but just as funny and as sad as it may sound, that's how we treat our life, every day making decisions and making choices. We are robbing ourselves. For example, everybody knows about the dangers of smoking and how this addiction takes the minutes, and then hours of life, but people still stubbornly steal their own lives, abruptly ending it. For example, eating foods with a high percentage of fat, we rob ourselves. Although we don't want to spend money on vitamin complexes. On the contrary, it's a pity we can easily neglect our health because we cannot afford to spend a certain amount on ourselves, or our health, choosing not life, but our wallet.

It turns out that over a lifetime a person gets comfortable living a certain way but loses the most important point of his life. A strange perception of life is that we are afraid of death, but at the same time doing

everything to bring it closer. The material acquisition makes us blind to what will happen after death. We buy apartments, homes, make repairs, and buy jewelry and other necessary things. But, where will it all be after we die? Can we take it with us into a real life after death? And, one more question: living with comfort and material goods, are you the one who holds your life? In fact, you do not? Then where will you be after your death?

Man does not live a hundred years, but bustling like thousand. In pursuit of worldly goods, we forget that we came into this world naked and we can't take anything with us when we leave it.

**As they say: «The last shirt has no pockets»
author unknown**

Death has no deposit account, and the tomb has no pockets. All that bustling is not for the sake of life, but to die in comfort. Is it worth to spend your life, and not to start living? We deceive ourselves when we think: right now I feel good, I have money, so I really live. Today you are young but will you be like that in 30 years? Today, you are rich but will you be rich tomorrow? Today you live, but will you have this life tomorrow? You acquire and acquire, but will it ensure that you get to Heaven after death?

Yes, it's hard to live for something greater than what we see daily, especially when we do not have the slightest understanding of Heaven. How many of us when we look

at the sky, see something more than a vast expanse of clouds and blue, and see more than just the colors and shades of the clouds? Does anyone of you see real life in this? Well, let's try to draw a picture of Heaven, based on the way it was seen by those who have visited it.

In the book of John Myers' "Voice from the Edge of Eternity,» this describes the feelings of a woman who also visited Heaven. As soon as her soul left her body, it fell into a place bathed in light. She believes that all Earthly pleasures are not comparable with what she experienced there.

The indescribable joy experienced by a woman, tells us that everything we enjoy here on Earth is a semblance of what could be true joy, what we will enjoy in Heaven. This is something that we can only experience from some external stimuli, but this joy in Heaven will be called everything that we can see and hear. It's part of life, thoughts; it's what pushes you to action, joy and love. While living on earth, we think that joy is when we get what we want, but it's a momentary satisfaction, that's all. In Heaven its part of our life, words, and actions.

Her soul reveled in the beauty, constantly feeling the presence of harmony, joy, compassion, she wanted to merge, to become a part of this beauty. Around her were trees covered with fruits and fragrant flowers, and she wanted to play with the crowd of children in the apple orchard.

The body in Heaven is characterized by beauty, and it became part of this woman's life. Everything that was inside her mind was harmony and joy. There was no fear or regret for life on Earth, there was no desire to go back. All she felt was that she has become part of the beauty of life itself. Heaven is as real as the Earth. We see the trees on Earth, but they are in Heaven, and they also bear fruit. It's real; like that today, you can eat apples from an apple tree. We receive flowers on some events, but in Heaven, these flowers are everywhere all year round and give a scent that cannot be enjoyed on Earth.

The woman saw the children, and that means that children also inherit Heaven. They are part of life in Heaven, as it is written in the Bible (Matthew 19:14): *"Let the little children come to me, and do not hinder them, for the kingdom of Heaven belongs to such as these."*

People who have been in paradise were impressed not only by its unearthly beauty, but also their feelings: a sense of serenity, universal love, and harmony. Perhaps this is the key moment of Heavenly bliss. The ability to love, give love to others is rewarded on Earth, and in Heaven, the souls immersed in the world of light and love, to dwell therein forever. (15)

I think that at this point our imaginations will draw a definite picture Heaven really looks like. I do not think anyone is interested in going where he does not have the slightest idea what awaits him there. No matter what you

have today, how wealthy you are, it is not worth a fraction of a percent if compared with the beauty of Heaven.

So today you can have the best of everything on Earth, but if you've never accepted Jesus as your Lord and Savior, you'll never inherit the real, fascinating life in Heaven. Here are the words of Omar Khayyam about the true wealth that is hidden not in the external possessions, but in how we live our lives on Earth.

It's good if your cloth is without a gap
And, it's not a sin to think about a daily bread,
And, you don't need anything else
Life is more precious than Earthly wealth.

What do we need to pay attention to? Is it the accumulation of external or internal acquisitions? The choice is always ours. Truly, Jesus Christ said in the Sermon on the Mount, what should not bother people, *"Do not store up for yourselves treasures on Earth, where moths and vermin destroy, and where thieves break in and steal. But, store up treasures for yourselves in heaven, where moths and vermin do not destroy, and where thieves do not break in and steal. For where your treasure is, there your heart will also be".*

Summary. *Nobody has the right to make us any richer or poorer, only ourselves.* We rob our health, steal our time hanging out aimlessly through life, we steal from people close to us when expecting something from them. . So we waste our years, and at the end, we understand that we have

robbed ourselves. The only thing that would be, is the realization that death is not the end but only the beginning of life. And it is a shame that for many there will be no point of return.

A German philosopher Immanuel Kant says: « **Give a man everything he wants, and at that moment, everything will not be everything"**. This is indeed the case if a person has no moral value and spends all his life accumulating external resources. Even acquiring all the riches of the world, he will remain poor because the enjoyment of life does not depend on comfortable living conditions, but from an internal feeling, cultivating values that reflect the love of God and people.

Summary. *Our life has its appeal, and its highest value is when someone receives something from us, that is, to serve others, not ourselves.*

LIVE RIGHT TODAY, NOT TOMORROW

Meet John as we study his life.
A blond tall guy about thirty years old. In his village, he was known as Kish, since he was very lanky and skinny. This did not detract him from his credibility. The whole village knew that if Kish gives a task, it must be done without delay, and no matter which way. Because they can be punished. Everyone implicitly listened to the village leader, pleasing any of his ideas and tasks. It felt it'll always be like that. But, life has made its own adjustments.

Since our hero was so cool, he was beginning to allow alcohol and soft drugs into his life. Rather this was just the beginning. Neither John (Kish) nor his friends thought about what will happen tomorrow, they said: «All is yet to come!» Laughing in the face of others, they gradually became addicted. And, within two years, all the «elite» of the village died. Every six months they buried another young boy who died of a drug overdose, and did not begin to live; they didn't expect such an end.

How do you like this story? I find it very unpleasant, especially since the guys were not some society outcasts, many of them were children of rich parents, and they had their own families. Yet, it did not define the outcome of their lives, with no expectations for the future, there actions daily led to disastrous consequences. The outcome of the story is logical because the guys lived the way they wanted, not the way they should.

Often we know what is good and what is bad, but make a choice of what we want, not how we should live. For example, a young man dreams of becoming rich, but he works little, sleeps a lot and spends money at night. He understands exactly that kind of lifestyle will never lead him to financial well-being, and it's his desire to live that way, and this draws him deeper into the cycle of poverty. Who is to blame in this scenario of life? The person making the choices. We determine how we live and what choices to make today. Do you want to live right? It's time to treat life as the most precious gift, start to appreciate every day, hour,

minute of your life. Want to live as it suits you it is also your choice. You may not think about what will happen after your death, but there is one event that is sure to happen and this is death. And, where will you spend your eternity? It is your responsibility according to the choice you have made today.

In one of the cases described by a man who «died» and went to Heaven. The first thing he felt was liberation from the body and arrival at the place, bathed in abundant light flowing from the open window into Heaven. «What I saw there made all the Earthly pleasures fade. I wanted to join the happy crowd of children, singing and frolicking in the apple orchard ... there were fragrant flowers and ripe red fruit on the trees. I sat there; reveling in the beauty and gradually began to feel the presence of joy, harmony,and compassion. My heart has sought to become a part of that beauty.»

Fifteen minutes later, he returned to his body, and that different world during the rest of his life was far more real than this one, which he returned to.

The feeling of living in Heaven was so deep and real, he did not want to go back to Earth, hoping to become a part of all this beauty. And, here we are, afraid of death, thinking that there is nothing better than life on Earth. It is absurd that we let fear lead us, making it impossible for us to live today for Heaven, making us spend our Earthly time, only for pleasure and satisfaction of our desires.

We can live as we fit, but must not fail to ask ourselves one question: «What's next?» It is our choice to answer or leave it unanswered, it also presents us with the opportunity to evaluate our past life. I will give an example showing the same question been answered by different people. This question is the latest in an interview, led by Vladimir Pozner (Soviet and Russian television journalist, TV anchorman), and it sounds like this: «Faced with God, what will you tell Him?» And this is what celebrities responded:

I.A. Urgent «*And what's next?*»

A.S. Konchalovsky: «*I did not know that You are real!*»

V.A. Tretiak: «*I'll thank him for my fate, I'm a happy man.*»

D. I. Kobzon: «*The last forgive me.*»

A.G. Gordon: «*I do not believe.*»

N.S. Mikhalkov: «*Lord, forgive me for being unable to love You the way You loved me.*»

A.B. Dzhigarkhanyan: «*I did not realize what I was doing.*»

Vladimir Zhirinovsky: «*I did everything I could, send me back; I will continue to struggle with what is there. I need a ticket back. I do not want to live here in paradise.*»

S. S. Govorukhin: «*Apologize. I would say that I had never believed that you existed in human form. I never believed in it.*»

Sting: «*What a surprise!*»

N. M. Tsiskaridze: «*I tried to live honestly in the name of God.*»

I. Ohlobystin: «*All I could ...*»

K.A. Rankin: «*Lord, I am glad, You are. I'm so happy. Sometimes I was afraid that you do not exist, sometimes it seemed to me that You don't, I'm sorry. "*(16)

Different people, different answers, but the bottom-line is that everyone will have something to say, and it should not be words of excuses; for some it will be the word of joy for life, and for someone else regrets that living for so long, he did not do anything for God. And in the end, it turned out that we were busy for ourselves, our desires, comfort, at the same time thinking that we acquired something. In fact, all that we have gained on Earth will stay here on Earth. Each of us must understand that our words do not justify or determine our eternity. Those who didn't reconcile with the Creator throughout their life, or simply were afraid to die and live for themselves, or tried to keep all that they had, doing nothing for other people, Hell awaits. Therefore, no matter what wise arguments you brought to people around, no matter how proven their desire to live in dignity before

God, the Lord will say His last word. And, His answer will determine our place in eternity.

If there is no God, and I believe in Him, I lose nothing. But, if God is there, and I don't believe in Him I'm losing everything.

Blaise Pascal,
(French mathematician, physicist, Religious philosopher and writer)

The truth is that we do not lose anything if we believe in God; on the contrary, we gain. We gain life, and thereby renounce Hell. When we find God, we give up the fear of death, seeing it as an acquisition of life. We get health, confidence, and joy, also knowing that no difficulty can stop us because we know that the one who gave us life is with us, he is our strength. Therefore, to Him what are our difficulties?

If we do not believe and rely only on ourselves, then what, people can change? Only what we understand. For example, if we have battled a virus, we run to the pharmacy, buy pills and we treat our health and then you need to treat the side effects of the drugs, which are taken because of the virus. In short, we treat the consequences of what we treated, undermining the health of the body. But, the situation can be changed if we believe: pray and ask God to recede the disease, help us with the treatment and restore the process of health fast.

Don't know how to get a guiding line to life? God took care of His children here, leaving us daily and timely instructions to life through the Holy Scriptures and the Bible. Therefore, if you do not know how to get an answer from God, or how to find a way out of any situation that arises in your life, read the New Testament. Jesus Christ is our example of life, he teaches us how to act and acquire a solid foundation of our spiritual values in life, overcoming the fear of death by faith and the life of Jesus Christ paid for every one of us.

Believing in God, we do not lose anything because we do not move away from the source of life. It's like a tree that is useful and alive as long as it feeds the root, but cut off the root from it, the tree will wither. If you plant a tree without roots in the ground, it'll stand for some time, and at first, no one will understand that it is lifeless. Also, such a tree, even if it has green leaves and branches, sooner or later they dry out and still fall. Likewise, people who do not have roots in their faith and service to God and people will fall. They will loose the possibility of gaining eternity in Heaven.

Do you know the source of your life? What gives you the confidence in life? What do you fill your life with? Answer honestly, you have to understand that many pretend to live, they even look like they are living, but the source of life within them is not there. There are people that are beautiful, but dead inside. Examine yourself by answering the aforementioned questions, and it won't be difficult to predict what will happen after death.

We rarely think about death, we don't question what's next, and how you need to live so that we won't justify our actions before God, and only thanking Him for life.

Summary. *To thank Heaven, you have to live today and tomorrow, and all those years you are meant to and don't hide from life, don't fear death.*

Overcoming the fear of death and not living with it is:

To appreciate every minute, knowing that a high price was paid for it - the life of Jesus Christ.

Appreciate other people, regardless of their status and position, knowing that God does not love someone more or less, and we are all equal before Him.

Creating spiritual values in our lives and acting based on principles such as respect, love, and humility

In order to have a tomorrow to look forward to, live for today so that tomorrow can come. To have a chance of getting to Heaven and enjoy its beauty, you need to lead a life worthy of such an honour.

But many live life casually, saying to themselves: «Let me enjoy my life, there is plenty of time!» The main thing is that «plenty of time» may be just your illusions which are very deceitful because death comes without giving you a notice.

Joke

From a conversation with children:

- How do people die?

- The stork carries them away.

Do not let it be said that «the Stork took you» without your knowledge.

Summary. *We only have today to live tomorrow. Do not count on "then", do not make promises on "someday", we have only today.* We have a prototype of Heaven on Earth so that we can live right in order to get a life in Heaven after death, and not the pain of disappointment in Hell.

We can live and enjoy life, and not be bored in Heaven, where there is everything. The word «all» refers to what we can see on Earth, but it is worth remembering that the Earth is a pathetic copy of what awaits us in Heaven.

For example, if, while living here on Earth, we want to go anywhere. We spend time, money, personal resources, while in Heaven it will be possible to do so with the very thought. If you have never seen Africa, for example, with just a thought you will find yourself in a place totally like Africa, and it is all you'll need. And, that is not the limited opportunities that you can afford on Earth that's all you want. But, more detail about this will be discussed later. Now I suggest we summarize this chapter:

1. People are not perfect, but this should not justify our irresponsibility. With daily routines and actions, it's necessary to strive to change, to become not better than anyone, but better than who we were yesterday. Life in Heaven doesn't depend on our desires, it is based on the motives of the heart and daily acts. However, it is worth remembering that we can only get to Heaven when we are reconciled with Jesus. We all have a chance to go to Heaven, and not only decision will take us there. Jesus is the way. Jesus says: «**I am the way, the truth, and the life. No one comes to the Father except through Me.**» There is only one way to Heaven, no other way exists. Therefore, we should not serve ourselves in this life, but the One who gave us this life: God our Creator.

2. By purchasing goods on Earth, building a life around our personal comforts, or creating comfort just for one's family, we do not get admission into Heaven. All we need to do is to love God and to create good deeds to help other people in order to make Heaven after a temporary life on Earth. After death, we take nothing and no one, it's just us. We will individually stand to be judged and answer for ourselves. What's the point in buying a car, if you did not help anyone with it or give them a ride? With all the money in your many bank accounts; who did you help, who lived in your big house? Yes, it is good to have the resources; but still they should not serve as personal comfort but they should become answers for others.

3. All the things and events that we put off until tomorrow may never be fulfilled for one reason: tomorrow may never come in your life. We need to live right today, remembering that we may not have "tomorrow" and the next year in our lives. We have to live right while being on Earth, to obtain Heaven.

4. Make haste to live for today, not the way you want, but the way you should. It is pointless just talking about the problems and turmoil around us; it is necessary to see the problems of the society, city, country, and to become the answer to these problems. When you do these, the solution to your problems will surely come.

GOLDEN TRUTH

• Live every day with gratitude, regardless of the circumstances occurring in your life; this is the joy of life.

• We are imperfect.

• Agreeing with your imperfections and not working on yourself is a sign of an irresponsible attitude to life.

• Life is in the hustle of every day, but it does not belong to us.

• In life, there are certain events that we have no control over, but we are still responsible for responding well to these events.

• We fuss not to get a life, but to die in comfort knowing that we have lived life the way it should.

• It is necessary to see the beauty of Heaven, and not just your apartment or car. No matter what you have on Earth today, how wealthy you are it is not worth a fraction of a percent compared with the beauty of Heaven.

• Life brings the greatest pleasure when someone receives something from you; In other words, the purpose of life is to serve others, not yourself.

• Even with the knowledge of what is good and what is bad, we must decide what to choose the right way or the wrong way.

• All that we see on the Earth is just a pathetic copy of what awaits us in Heaven.

TEST
«ILLUSION
OF VISIBLE ACQUISITION»

In each statement or question of the test, there should be only one answer. Next to each answer, in brackets, is a score. Your result of the test corresponds to the obtained amount of points.

1. Looking at the sky, what do you think about?
a) It is beautiful (1)
b) I have no time to look around (0)
c) It is good that there is a sky, it is the law of nature (1)
d) It makes me think about life (2)
e) I dream of living in Heaven (3)

2. If you see an old man begging, will you stop to help him?
a) I'm always in a hurry, so I won't stop (1)
b) I don't pay attention to these people (0)
c) They beg because they like it, I know such people ... (1)
d) I will help the old man next time (2)
e) I will offer my help right away, even if I have no money (3)

3. Are you ashamed of the misdeeds in your life? Do you blame yourself for this?
a) No, I don't, I live the way I want (1)
b) I am living in constant self-depreciation (0)
c) I try not to think about it. It is what it is, I have reconciled (1)
d) Yes, and I forgive myself for the misdeeds (2)
d) Every day I strive to be better than I was yesterday (3)

4. What do you spend most of your income on?
a) On myself (1)
b) The food and clothing (0)
c) I do not know where the money goes to (1)
d) More on my needs, but I try to help family too (2)
e) The money is invested in personal development and in affecting people positively (3)

5. How often do you stop your desires, knowing that they won't bring you any good?
a) No, life is good, because I live the way I want (1)
b) Never, I do what I like (0)
c) I think rationally, but sometimes allow myself to relax (2)
d) I am guided not by the wishes but my heart (3)

RESULTS
OF THE TEST

Less than 5 points. Unfortunately, you live for temporary pleasure, which is based on your desires. Moreover, these desires are valid only in the present day, and you do not think about what awaits you later on. You are wasting your life.

6-9 points. You are responsible for your life partially - when you control the situation, there are good results, but once you are relaxed, you lose control of the situation. Hence, you live well than bad. This unfortunately, does not bring you closer to Heaven. You should not be that cold, and then hot in your life, you need to decide how you want to live, and aspire to live like that. I think this book will help you.

10-15 points. Life for you is an opportunity to become important in the life of another person. You are trying to responsibly approach the important decisions. You are motivated to live in Heaven, considering it as a primary outcome thereby bringing you closer to your desired daily activities, not only to yourself but also to others. Sometimes you feel uncomfortable, but doesn't affect you or your feelings, your goal is to live on Earth for Heaven.

PRACTICAL
TASKS

1. Close your eyes and draw a picture of the outcome of your life. Imagine that you are giving a report for the years you already lived. What do you see now? Write what you felt, what surprised you, and how you see the outcome of your life on Earth.

2. Perform the first point of the task, imagine, to what extent and scale you would like to reproduce the years of your life. Begin to see the people who have helped you, remember who they are, where they live and what they do. Write down your expectations of life.

3. Make a daily plan for implementing your actions to have an effect not as it does now, but an impact that will outlive you.

Recommended books of the UNIVERSITY of LIFE «Life is an opportunity.» Developing internal feeling of your personality, you will not be a bystander in life. But, obtaining will, character, you will be the leader of your life.

Chapter 5

OPENING THE CURTAIN OF HEAVEN

Chapter 5.
OPENING THE CURTAIN
OF HEAVEN

Everybody wants to go to Heaven, but nobody wants to die.

Joe Louis
An American professional boxer

We want to go to Heaven, but we don't want to leave this world. Sounds paradoxical, doesn't it? Still, it's quite simple: there is a fear of death, uncertainty about the future, disbelief in the Creator of life. But in spite of everything, deep down each one of us desires an eternity Heaven. In the previous chapter, we discussed the fact that you can obtain all the treasures here on Earth, all the riches of the world but this does not determine your path to Heaven. After the physical death, the good heart, with good deeds will spend eternity in Heaven.

Summary: OVERCOMING THE FEAR OF DEATH is possible if one will live not for self but for people. It doesn't matter if you think of Heaven or not, if you believe in God or not, that's all up to a certain time. After all, each of us had a moment when there was nobody except God, and we ask Him for help.

Unfortunately, the smell of money has surpassed the smell
of conscience. That's why so often we appeal to God only
on the deathbed.

Author Unknown.

Imagine you are flying in a plane and all of a sudden turbulence is encountered, this will create fear in your mind. Besides this, dozens of times you have seen movies with a plane crash or the lose of control during takeoffs or landings. In those moments, only very few people think about what to eat or what gift to buy their wives. The only thing that happens in such moments is experience of a great fear. In those moments, you realize that there is only God. What do you think people on a plane about to crash ponder about? They pray! They pray to God but pretend nothing happens. Therefore, it may be supposed that it is not your beliefs about faith that affirms your position but rather, the absence of answers to the vital questions.

THINGS ON EARTH JUST A SHADOW OF THINGS TO COME

*— The rage compresses the soul and a man gets blind.
Tell me, is it possible for an evil person to understand
Heaven?*
— Well, both good and evil can see it.
*— He will see it by sight, not by heart. He will look at it
and pass by. And he will die without understanding.*

Olga Ozertsova. "Vesnianka"

So the minutes, days, years of our life pass. We can see Heaven, the people, somebody's troubles, but we hurry, running mad, never becoming the answer to those who need us. And we live in such a way from day to day, from year to year, and we are missing the opportunities that could bring us closer to Heaven.

A doctor from Virginia, George Richie was admiring the pictures of paradise for a few moments. He saw the effulgent city, where everything was shining: the houses, the streets, walls, and the inhabitants of this world were also woven of light.

There are lights everywhere in the city. Everything is woven from light and it is really beautiful to see and understand that there is no obscurity, no darkness, and no fear in Heaven. There is only light that radiates everything

that is in Heaven - the people, the buildings, and roads. That is so wonderful to realize how beautiful it is in Heaven which is waiting for each of us. But do we see Heaven in our life, or just live in the illusions NOT HAVING TO OVERCOME THE FEAR OF DEATH?

So, is Heaven just what we can see with our own eyes? If so, why do we not look the same way at other things around us? Why having the phone when we do not use it? After all, we do not see all of its functions with our own eyes, do we? We have examined all the gadget's functions, we have rummaged in its assignment, and we have tried to use it. The same with Heaven: you should examine it and understand how the things there function, and how to use your time here on Earth to come closer to Heaven.

Summary. *Without seeking to learn what Heaven can be, we live our lives in vain.*

Let's try to draw a picture of our Earthly perception of what life in Heaven may be. Having an idea of the Earth, we assume that Heaven is something similar to what we see here every day. For example, a phone in its present form arose out of some ideas. After much development, testing, and proving and now becoming the most elaborate device it is today. The same way our Earth was created with a specific layout from someone's drafts. You have to understand that the phone is of man's handiwork while the Earth is God's creation. If the Earth is so perfect in proportion to the laws

of gravity, light, thermodynamics, and other essential items then imagine how perfect Heaven is.

Yes, there are different approaches to the question; who created the Earth; there is, for instance, the theory that our planet emerged as a result of the Big bang. But the following material will make you wonder if everything is so simple and everything we know emerged by itself, then why are we alone in the whole universe.

In 1966, Time magazine published a cover story, which asked the question: «Is God dead?» It turned out that the rumors about the death of God is premature. Most striking is the fact that the recent arguments in favor of His existence appeared in a very unexpected place — they were prompted by science.

The same year, when Time published a now famous article, an astronomer Carl Sagan said that there are two important criteria for the existence of extraterrestrial life. There should be a «right» star and a habitable planet must be at the correct distance from it. Considering the fact that there are around octillion planets in the Universe (one-thousand-ninth degree, or 1027), from which nearly about a septillion of them are livable (one-thousand-eighth degree, or 1024).

With a chance of success, they decided to launch in 1960, a collection of large and costly private and government projects on the search for extraterrestrial life it was very likely and very quickly supposed to give at least some result.

With the help of a vast network of radio telescopes, scientists listened to the Universe's sounds in search of signals that could resemble coded information and wouldn't be accidental. But, the years passed and the silence of the Universe was still deafening. In 1993, the Search for Extraterrestrial Intelligence program has been deprived of funding, but the search was continued with private funds. As of 2014, scientists have discovered no civilizations, after which was silence.

What have happened? By increasing our knowledge of the Universe, we began to realize that existence demands more factors than Sagan considered. His two parameters have increased from ten to twenty, then to fifty. The number of habitable planets decreased respectively; up to several thousand; and continues to decrease.

The number of parameters have continued to increase, and the number of planets has dropped to zero. In other words, the existence of livable planets in the whole Universe, including our own, has become impossible. Probability theory says that even our existence should not be possible.

Today there are approximately 200 known criteria for the existence of extraterrestrial life on other planets, and potentially habitable planets must comply with each of them without exception, otherwise the whole system will fall apart. If Jupiter wasn't so close to Earth sucking in meteorites with its powerful gravity then the Earth would suffer meteorites would fall to Earth a thousand times more. The chances of the existence of life in the Universe are remarkably little.

That's not all. That fine-tuning, which is necessary for the existence of life on the planet is nothing compared with the fine-tuning necessary for the existence of the Universe itself. For example, astrophysics knows that the values of the four fundamental interactions - gravitational, electromagnetic, as well as strong and weak nuclear interaction have been established less than a millionth of a second after the «Big Bang.» Change at least one value, and the Universe will no be able to exist. For instance, if the relationship between the strong nuclear force and the electromagnetic interaction has been changed at least a tiny fraction of negligible proportion, at least at 1/100,000,000,000,000, there would be no stars in Heaven.

Now multiply this single parameter for all other necessary conditions and you will get the chance of the Universe existence.

An astronomer by the name Fred Hoyle, who had coined the term «big bang», said that the data on the probability of the existence of life in the Universe has seriously undermined his atheistic beliefs. Later he wrote: «The interpretation of these facts on the basis of common sense suggests that super intelligence is just playing with physics, as well as with chemistry and biology ... The numbers of calculations based on these facts are so mind-boggling that this summary appears to me incontestable.»

A theoretical physicist by the name Paul Davies said: «The evidence of intelligent concept is tremendous"

and an Oxford professor by the name John Lennox, said: « The more we know about our Universe, the more convincing the hypothesis of the Creator's existence becomes in explaining the reasons for our existence».

The universe is the greatest phenomenon of all time. It is a miracle of miracles that inevitably, with all the power of shining stars, indicates the existence of something or someone — more than the Universe itself. (17)

Well, do we still argue or agree with the theoretical physicists? The Earth is not an accident, Heaven has a consistent pattern. Everything starts from something, and to grow a fruit, the seed is needed. But speaking of Heaven, I still want to show you how beautiful it is. For instance, our ability to see the colors of the world is a kind of preparation to enable us see the beauty of Heaven in all its unprecedented abundance of color. Sometimes we talk about an indefinite color, but in eternity, this or a similar color is possible, you can see and admire it. This fact has been repeatedly confirmed by eyewitnesses, who managed to visit Heaven.

The light of the Sun is only a visible part of what the beam may be. Everybody who's been in Heaven has talked about the softness and at the same time the brightness of that light. This light radiates all around, even on your body, and it is very pleasing to our eyes, so much that you do not want to take your eyes off that heat. For example, gold and jewels are given to us with only one purpose - to show that

they are only a small part of what God has prepared for us in Heaven. On the Earth, these jewels are not available for everybody in large quantities; hence, to indulge in buying gold or diamond jewelry, you must work for at least a month or even two. Someone even over a lifetime does not have the opportunity to buy such jewelry, seeing them only on the windows of jewelry shops. But imagine that in Heaven, even the streets are lined not with asphalt or stones but with gold, emeralds, and diamonds. Imagine you are walking down a path not covered with pebbles, but down the roads made of gold interspersed with diamonds, and your eyes, your whole body will enjoy the sight.

Do you have a house or apartment here on Earth? This means that each of us will have a house in Heaven. It will be different, with its unique beauty, with its colors and shades. A simple example is someone who writes music and it brings joy to an audience. In Heaven, we will hear the music in its entirety, not just hearing by ears, but with every fiber of our body. Here, on Earth, we have got just our ears as the organ of hearing, but in Heaven your eyes will hear, and your skin and hair. Everything that constitutes our body will feel, hear, see, and understand everything that is happening around us. In addition to this, you can only dream about something these days, but there is everything for those who live in Heaven.

The woman, who had fallen into a state of clinical death, at that very moment left her body. Standing beside the bed and seeing herself from the side, she felt the nurse

went through her, going to take the oxygen mask. Then she floated up, found herself in a tunnel, and went to the shining light. She was in a wonderful place, filled with bright colors, indescribable and not similar to those we have on Earth. All space was filled with brilliant light. There were so many happy people, some of them were lights too. In the distance, there was a city, with buildings, fountains and sparkling water ... It was filled with light. There were also happy people and beautiful music playing.

Here it is, the superiority of Heaven where everything is in harmony, light, and beauty. Where the people themselves are light, everything we see on Earth is seen also in Heaven but more perfect and much more grandiose in scale.

Summary. *Are you still afraid of dying? If so, then you will never begin living for Heaven.* That's why, all that we have, or see, or imagine in our fantasies here on Earth is a clue for us to what we will have in Heaven. All available joy will be given to us not for something, but just by proving the fact that we will live there. CONQUER THE FEAR OF DEATH by the clear representation of the beauty of Heaven, and then nothing will be able to take away what you live for.

IT CAN'T BE BORING IN HEAVEN

The Saint Salvius of Albi, the Gallic hierarchy of the VI century, came back to life after being dead most of the day,

and he told his friend Gregory of Tours the next words.

When my cell was shocked and you saw me dead, I was raised up by two angels and assigned to the highest summit of Heaven, and then under my feet not only this wretched Earth was seen, but also the sun, moon and stars. Then I was passed through the gate that shone brighter than the sun, and I entered the building where the floors gleamed with gold and silver. That was the light that is impossible to be described. I was greeted by some creatures, some of which were dressed in priestly vestments, and others - at the usual dress. Then a voice from the cloud said, «Let this man return to the Earth because the Church needs him.» After that, crying my eyes out, I went back through the gate, into which I had entered. (18)

According to the story of the priest, who had contact with Heaven just for an instant, the whole of our planet and the Universe turned out to be quite insignificant and small. Even with the continuation of his earthly life, with grief and tears, he parted with the fact that became part of his life after death. Today, we need to understand that the real, genuine life will begin only when the physical body dies and God will take us into His home. We have to live every moment of our life for eternity, and not to fear death, sitting in a «closet» and living a life for pleasure.

Today, in order to feel happiness and joy in our life on Earth, we rely on something that supports us, such as a desired gift, or an appointment, vacation, or holiday. After

our death, when we get into Heaven, all of this will no longer be needed. Every second of our lives there, we will feel happiness and joy, from the crown of our head to the sole of our feet, and it will last permanently. If your pleasure on Earth is temporary, dependent on external «gifts», the joy in Heaven will last forever.

If the feeling of joy and happiness last constantly and continuously in Heaven, then isn't this endless storm of emotions boring? No, it's not! After all, a sense of joy and love arises not only from the fact that we feel it, but also from all that we can see, hear, and experience. Imagine the possibility to communicate with flowers, which not just talk about their lives, but are able to carry on a dialogue on any topic. For example, how impeccable you are and how beautiful Heaven is. Everything that is in Heaven is like a guide for it. Flowers, trees, animals, and angels speak and show the beauty of Heaven. I am sure that there is no place for boredom where there is everything, including supernatural capabilities that are not available on the Earth.

Yes, thanks to technology, we have the opportunity to use the Internet, and it is available to almost everybody, but what about space? Only a lucky few have visited it, but personally, you, do you have such an opportunity? The inhabitants of Heaven go wherever they would like to and see parts of the Universe where they had never been before, and maybe even have not heard its name. We all cling to the limits of the city, not wishing to leave it, or without having such an opportunity. Are you still afraid of death?

Summary. *If you are afraid of death, you should give up this fear, appreciating the truth of life, which begins only after death.*

All that we possess here on the Earth is a deteriorated copy of what awaits us in Heaven, so let the fear of death go, replacing it with the advantages of living in Heaven.

Summary. *On the Earth, we suffer humiliation and defeat, and life challenges us more and more every day. In Heaven, there is only the enjoyment of all that surrounds us.* For instance, you have an expensive smartphone with super high-speed and multiple functions but you paid a lot of money or even took out a loan. If anything happens to your smartphone, you will lose the peace in your heart, your mood will turn sour, but in Heaven all the possibilities are progressive in millions of times, and without auxiliary means you can create the images that you wish to see around you, you can take pictures of everything you see, even micro-particles of air and water. Is it possible to get bored with such opportunities?

LIVING ON EARTH BRINGS THE POSSIBILITY TO GO TO HEAVEN

The streets were filled with the snow of December. The frost was rather mild, but the cold wind penetrated Susie to the bones. She quickly jumped out of the bus. She did not

like this time of the year: cold, dark, and damp, a time it seemed that warmth will never come. Again a part of the street lights were turned off, and she was forced not just to go faster, but to start jogging in the unlit areas.

Our heroine thought of hot tea and how her children will meet her. But, suddenly she saw a man lying near the store. She has passed him daily as she ran home. «What a drunkard … he is not even thinking about freezing and dying.»

Susie went on, but all of a sudden one thought stopped her: how many people have passed this man with the same thought about him? Having no idea how long he's been lying there, near this store. She quickly turned around and ran back. Leaning closer to the man, she began to inspect him. His hands were barely warm, and he was gradually returning to consciousness, then nodding off again, repeating one sentence: «I just want to sleep.» Susie woke him, telling him that he has to go home, that it's cold outside, and he just might die.

Nearby there were taxi drivers standing around, they saw a young girl who was carrying the adult man herself, and they were just scoffing, saying, «Leave that drunkard.» Nobody helped her or asked her what happened. Having found a phone in the man's pocket, Susie called the last incoming number and it was the number of his wife, who has been alone worrying.

As it turned out, the man simply happened to be in a totally unfamiliar city. He came here with a friend who had just abandoned him. Susie dragged the man to the bus stop, put him on a bus, and told his wife where she could meet him.

It seemed that it was the end, the man went home, but tears flowed down Susie's cheeks. Going home, she thought about what might have happened if she passed by and did not help a person in need.

Half an hour of your time can save someone's life. One dollar from your salary may prolong someone's life for a day. So, a lot or a little depends on us? I believe, in fact, more than we can imagine. Therefore, whether we live using our capabilities or are afraid to take risks is a life choice for each of us.

Summary. *The fear of death can be defeated when you value the life of another person and do everything possible to serve others.*

During our life on Earth, God is testing us on:

- the strength of our decisions

- the strength of our responsibility

- the strength of our love for people

You may ask: what is it for? I will answer you. God is doing this in order to invite you to a life of pleasure, guided by the fact that whether you have done something for others, whether you have served someone in your life. We have enough to be needed by someone. Each of us has a lifetime and what we spend it on, will determines our path after death.

God Himself invites us to the feast of life in Heaven, but for some reasons it is important for us to hold on to an earthly copy of this life, thinking that the Earth is a true place for spending our lives. We invite guests for holidays on the assumption of how valuable a gift they can bring us, whether our relationships are close or not, whether we like the judgments of potential candidates, whether we are satisfied with their appearance. God is not a hypocrite, he is not the respecter of persons and he loves everyone. Hence, He has prepared Heaven for all of us, but the way we live on the Earth will determine whether we will be invited into Heaven or not. This is why, our earthly life should abound in daily actions, not only to our own advantage but also helping people whom we are obliged to teach, living the way we do. In other words, doing everything for others remembering that life in Heaven is for eternity.

Summary. *We are afraid of losing something that is temporary and transitory, but at the same time, do not seek to acquire something that is eternal even after our death - a life in Heaven.*

So what really lies behind this simple word «Heaven»? What do people learn through their whole life? What do they lose, restricting their lives, seeing only the visible? This is discussed in the next chapter, first let's summarize the current.

1. All that we have on the Earth gives us a hint about what Heaven might be. We shouldn't limit the benefits of Heaven only by our assumptions. You are not a human that creates life. You can bear a baby, but you do not specify which body or even the color a baby's eyes will be. And, the entire process of emergence of a new life is perfect, starting with the first cells of the body and ending with pregnancy and birth. If God has set this complex process for the birth of a new life, do you really think that the Earth is all that God is capable of? Of course not. In its perfection, Heaven surpasses the Earth a million times because that is where the Creator lives.

2. All that we want to live for is in Heaven and if you're happy to live life on Earth, Heaven will be an incredible discovery for you, full of opportunities and prospects. Bored is the one who is not able to appreciate every moment of their life, who ignores the hints of Earth and lives only a mundane life. Living in this way, we neglect our lives.

3. Each day lived on the Earth is an opportunity to come closer to Heaven and it's a fascinating feature. So every day we describe Heaven with our words, actions, and doings. But if we are able to get a place in it, it will be determined by the quality of our past days, whether they were lived in serving people or for our own pleasure.

GOLDEN TRUTH

• It is not our perishable wealth but the abundance of our good deeds that will show the prospects of our stay after the physical death

• Having not understood Heaven at least at a fraction of a percent, we live our life in vain

• Everything that we have on Earth is just a copy of what awaits us in Heaven, and believe me, THERE IS NO PLACE FOR BOREDOM IN HEAVEN

• There is only enjoyment of everything which surrounds you in Heaven

• Life on Earth is limited by ourselves in particular, and by our means as well, but there is no money and greed for wealth in Heaven, there is only one thing - LOVE

• The feeling of happiness in Heaven will be permanent, we will always experience it

• It does not matter how old are you, the only thing that matters is what you have done today for those who are around you

• Live today as if tomorrow may never come

• Life on Earth is the way God is testing us and the strength of our solutions, the responsibility, and the strength of love for other people

• The beauty of Heaven He has prepared for each of us, but the way we live on the Earth will determine whether we will enter Heaven after our life on Earth.

TEST
"THE THIRST FOR LIFE IN HEAVEN"

In each statement or question of the test, there should be only one answer. Next to each answer, in brackets, is a score. Your result of the test corresponds to the obtained amount of points.

1. What do you think about in moments of fear; the safety or the possibility of coming closer to God?
a) I'm just afraid, and that's all (1)
b) I do not think at all (0)
c) I think about the family, the children, how they would cope without me (1)
d) I think about my actions and its motives (2)
e) I come closer to God in praying (3)

2. You are going down the street and hear someone crying out loud, how will you react?
a) I do not care, I am in a hurry (1)
b) I will wonder, what have happened? (0)
c) I will say to myself someone is suffering again (1)
d) I would go to find out what have happened, I will question those who are near (2)
e) I will offer assistance (3)

3. Have you ever had a dream about life in Heaven?
a) No, it is unreal (1)
b) It is too early, I am young ... (0)
c) No, I am not worthy of it (1)
d) I dream about it, but I am not sure whether I
   will get it (2)
e) I live for Heaven (3)

4. What determines your eternity in Heaven?
a) A desire (1)
b) A fortune (0)
c) Constellation of circumstances (1)
d) Thoughts and desires (2)
e) Daily good deeds (3)

5. Does your life on Earth bring you joy?
a) Of course, I live for my pleasure (1)
b) Everything irritates me (0)
c) I do not know, it depends on my mood (1)
d) It brings me joy, especially when it's my
   personal decision (2)
e) Of course, I am happy and grateful for everything
   I already have (3)

RESULTS
OF THE TEST

Less than 5 points. You should think about your life, not only your desires, but in the context of your future. Everything you do in your life is vain. But sooner or later it will come to end, and you could simply have no time to think about your eternity.

6-9 points. You live an ordinary life, so to speak: you live the way the others live. Still, in moments of despair, you realize that there is something much more than just your desires or beliefs. I think this book will help you make the right decision and recognize the creator of your life; God.

10-15 points. Heaven is your goal. This is what you seek in accordance with your daily activities and actions. You realize that sooner or later you will have to give an account of your life. Continue serving people by all means.

PRACTICAL TASKS

1. How many times during the day do you catch yourself wishing to become the answer to someone's life problem?

2. Write down the circumstances under which you will not ignore the needs of the other person.

3. What prevents you from aspiring to a life in Heaven?

4. Write down three new decisions which have crossed your mind after reading this chapter.

Recommended Book of UNIVERSITY OF LIFE - «How to live to a hundred percent». Everyday life brings us to the account for our years, days of life. By defining life as a high-quality product and seeing the impact of life on Earth, you will bring yourself closer to the beauty of Heaven.

Chapter 6

IMAGE
OF HEAVEN
ON EARTH

Chapter 6.
IMAGE
OF HEAVEN ON EARTH

How long does it take to create a memory of a person? An hour of the marble's work.

Allen Carr, smoking-fighter, founder of the worldwide network of Easyway To Stop Smoking Clinics

We can live so that after the death of the body we can enjoy life in Heaven. But we often fuss, fuss, and fuss without seeking answers to what our tomorrow will be. We think only about what we have today, and hope that it will last forever. But, really, only one hour's work of a marbler is enough to keep the memory of a man. It may sound too sarcastic or rude, but this is true. Is it only the fear of death that can make us reconsider our way of life, all the legacy of which will be written on the tombstone. After all, what brings back the memory of your grandfathers and grandmothers to the second or third generation? It is usually only pictures or monuments on their graves. But there are those who «have raised a monument not built with hands.» So, the way we spend the years of our lives on Earth determines where we spend eternity. A pressing question arises: WHAT WILL HAPPEN AFTER DEATH? Do not think that life will end only inside a grave at the cemetery?

For some, death becomes an incredible preoccupation in Heaven, and for others, an eternity in Hell.

Having an opportunity to explore Heaven, we must understand that everything that surrounds us is an image of Heaven on Earth. Even the fact that we have children is just a lesson for us about what it means to have a family relationship, what empathy is, and how these feelings should serve not us, but the needs of others. All that we have on Earth is a mirror image of Heaven on Earth, everything is perfect there, and Heaven contains opportunities for a true life. There is also no sin in Heaven or the battle to conquer the flesh.

AROMA FROM THE KITCHEN

All that we see, what does it tell us about? For what purpose do we use all that surrounds us? Or are we just consumers, living by a rule: «We must make maximum use of everything»?

Seeing the Earth and not thinking of Heaven is the same as having a kitchen where your favorite dish is cooking, and not being able to enter it. You smell the aroma, you know what delicacy is about to be made ready, but you do not go there for one simple reason: you are simply afraid. You give way to doubt, you're not confident in your decision, you have second thoughts. The same with life after death: we hear about the advantages of Heaven, we have at least once in our life heard a phrase like, «Just do not go to Hell!» So,

we already have some knowledge about the afterlife, about the existence of Heaven and Hell, but still we have doubts.

Here is the testimony of a 15 year old girl, her name is Jennifer Perez. She was raised in a Christian family. But it just so happens that she abandoned her faith and became involved in drugs. When she was dying of an overdose, she was sent to Hell. Fortunately, she was given a second chance and a mission to go back and warn the others.

When I woke up, I felt my spirit leaving my body. I was in a hospital and saw my doctors and nurses gathered around my body. When I came out of my body, I saw it lying on the bed. It's as if you look at your reflection in the mirror. But I saw not the reflection, but my body on the bed. When I turned around, I saw two people dressed in red. They said, «Come with us» - and grabbed me by the arms. They brought me to a place, and when I looked around, I realized that this was Heaven!

I looked ahead and saw the Father. I could not see his face because of the glory surrounding Him. It was so great, so bright; it beamed and filled Heaven with its light. There was no sun, no moon, no stars, He was the light.

The absence of the sun, moon, and stars, gives us a clue that in Heaven there is no day or night, which means that time is static there, it is everlasting. So, we have to understand that our life on Earth is predetermined by time and years of life, but after death, we have an eternity in

Heaven or in Hell. Living in the glory of God will be for eternity as well as pain and burning of the sinful. It also does not last a year or two, but eternity.

When I stood in front of the Father, I felt very dirty! I fell to my knees and cried. I was very ashamed. Even if I could see His faces, I would not want to, because I was so ashamed. When I stood before the Lord, He showed me a movie of my life from the beginning until now. He told me that what is most important is what I will do after my salvation.

When I stood in front of Him on my knees, I cried not being able to stop. I still did not want to look in His face, because I was very ashamed of myself. But the Lord in such a sweet and gentle voice said to me: «I love you.» In exactly the same way, He loves you. But then He said this to me personally. He said that he forgave me for all that I have done, including offenses against Him. He forgave me!

He told me that I have a mission, and it is to tell all the young people about my vision. Even if I do not want to do that, I will do it because the Lord commanded me so.

When I returned to my body, I woke up and found myself in the hospital. I looked around and saw the droppers, devices measuring the beating of my heart, various tubes. Soon my parents visited me, and I began to cry. They looked very angry, but the Lord ordered me to tell them everything. That's what I did. I told them everything. (19)

We must understand one thing: Heaven and Hell, are not fairy tales supposed to amuse or frighten us, they are both continuations of our earthly life. As it is proven that death is just a continuation and our transition from one state to another, it means that the choice of where to spend eternity depends on us. There is a choice to live today so as to inherit eternity in Heaven, or to live and think that one day later in old age, we will change our lives, repent and not go to Hell. Good for you, if you make it in time. But remember that a person dies in the world every second.

There is no doubt that the soul exists and it is in our body. The body dies, and this is a normal process, the soul leaves the body, and this was proven. But what happens later is not luck, it's your choice today whether to believe in the reality of Heaven or to refute it as a questionable fact.

Doubts or fears arise for one simple reason: you have not studied the question fully. You just have not formed your answers; have not made up your mind on the basis of the analysis and research on this topic. Here are the consequences of the seemingly innocuous doubts.

1. You are irresponsible. If you are not interested in what directly concerns your life, do you really want to say that you might be interested in the life or actions of another person? You are not a solution neither for the people nor for society, you are the problem.

2. You lack initiative. Putting it bluntly, you are lazy. You are not interested in the future of your life, you live only with what you already have, and find it difficult to go beyond your interest. It's kind of limp agreement with those situations that come into your life and not the situation that you have to create yourself.

3. You are careless. You do not care about the consequences of your actions. You have accepted the position of «come what may, and for now dance»? It is the bane of our youth - «I live the way I want and I enjoy life.» Go the cemetery, and look at the age at which people died in the past year. The picture is not a pleasant one: there are much more people under 40years old buried than those over 70years old.

4. You are frivolous. You do not have any position or stand, you are focused on your mood. You may have good thoughts but then you change your mind easily. You are so unreliable, so easily influenced by other people's opinion, this is even without analyzing a situation and drawing personal conclusions.

5. You are short-sighted. Such people do not care about their future and show the same example to their children. Not thinking ahead today, not foreseeing what awaits them, how their children will live, what society will be like, you float down the river of life. Unfortunately, this current carries you through life without your intervention.

Still uncertain about what will happen after your death, even «smelling the aroma from the kitchen,» you will consider going there or not? But if you do not eat, the body will be weakened, and this will lead to death. Do you still have doubts about the existence of Heaven? But if you do not explore it, you will never get there.

Often in the street someone approaches us, says something, but we do not pay attention, missing the opportunity to hear for one simple reason: too busy with ourselves. Our friends may go to church, tell us about the spiritual values, but it is easier to perceive them as sectarian or fanatical than afford to hear «kitchen aroma», learn about the opportunities of Heaven. People are too busy with mundane chores, but at the same time absolutely do not care about the important things of their life, and only, when faced with the fear of death because of illness or circumstances, they start to think about their eternity.

Suppose we condemn mothers who abandon their newborn children on the streets or, at best, let them in the hospitals after birth. We say, «Indeed, it is so bad, how could she have done such a thing!» But we ourselves refuse the Creator of life, the One, Who gave us this life, and when someone talks about Him, we snort and do not want to hear. So why don't we condemn ourselves and understand that we are giving up on our Father? Because we are too busy with our personal lives.

Doubts are the information we reject, the facts we do not accept or do not try to analyze.

Meet the first man in space, Yuri Gagarin. His name may only be heard in the former Soviet Union or in space flights.

There are many streets and schools named in honor of the first cosmonaut in the world. But his death in 1968 was the source of the same number of conspiracy theories.

The bare facts about the tragedy that happened not far from Moscow, March 27, 1968, were made public long ago. Gagarin and his flight instructor Vladimir Seregin performed a routine test flight in the MiG-15 in poor weather conditions. They have successfully completed the planned maneuvers and were already heading for the runway when radio contact with the aircraft suddenly cut short. Later, rescuers found the remains of MiG on the bottom of a deep crater in the forest. Both pilots were dead, and their bodies severely disfigured. Gagarin was only 34, and at the time of his premature death, he was the most likely candidate to lead the Soviet expedition of the moon landing (in what Americans were ahead of the USSR in 1969).

It seemed like his plane went into the «black peak», out of which was able to come, and the pilots apparently lost control. They established a government commission to investigate the death of Chevalier of the Order of Lenin and Hero of the Soviet Union.

Upon hearing the news, people in the Moscow underground were crying. Thousands of people for several days were standing in commemoration line to his ashes. About two hundred experts, participated in the investigation. The head of state Leonid Brezhnev banned publication of the results and put the 30-volume report on a shelf. Investigators were forbidden to publish their Summaries on the pretext that it may «upset» the country, and soon the case was forgotten. (20)

You may wonder the use of this story. But here are some interesting facts about the hero of our story.

After returning from spaceflight, Yuri Gagarin said, «I was in interplanetary space and I did not see God. So, there is no God.» Some people took that statement as true, alleging that modern science supposedly disproves the existence of God. Others, seeing that Gagarin may not have had even reached the moon, have concluded that he unlikely had the right to declare that he had examined all the space.

On the basis of this very naive reasoning of the deceased Gagarin, it must be said that his words can be taken for truth only by people who intentionally reject God. In contrast, the first group of American astronauts, who reached the moon and made a landing there, read the first verse of the first chapter of the Bible in the orbit of the moon and passed on this reading via the television network to the entire world. This indicated their faith that «In the beginning God created the Heaven and the Earth.» (21)

Word of doubt, and in the case of Yuri Gagarin, in general, his assertion, was destructive. In addition, we must take into account the strength of its impact on the minds of the Soviet people: they saw him as a hero, trusting his every word as the highest authority. In this way, Yuri Gagarin has taken up the mission to publicly conclude whether there is a God or not. If we deny the Father and His existence, then we by our own choice get away from His protection and coverage. In light of the above, does it not seem strange that people are afraid of death because they live without God, without His protection and, therefore, know that after death on Earth the eternal death in Hell is waiting for them.

So much for the «aroma from the kitchen»: we smell it, we know about it, but are trying to contradict it because of our negligence, selfishness, ignorance, and disrespect for the Creator of life.

A VIEW OF EARTH THROUGH THE DIM GLASS

One barber, trimming his client's hair, is talking to him about God:

— If God exists, why are there are so many sick people? Why are there street children and unjust wars? If he really existed, there would be neither suffering nor pain. It is hard to imagine a loving God who allows all this. Therefore, I personally do not believe in his existence.

Then the client said to the barber:

— You know what I say? Hairdressers do not exist

— How come? – The barber wondered. - One of them now stands in front of you.

— No! – The client exclaimed. - They do not exist; otherwise, there would be no overgrown and unshaven men as the man over there who is walking down the street.

— Well, good man, it's not about the barbers! People simply do not come to me.

— There you have it! – his client confirmed. - My point is the same: God exists. People simply do not seek Him and do not come to Him. That is why there is so much pain and suffering in the world.

That's how sometimes we, like the barber, look at things with our own eyes, our sight is aimed only at ourselves and at what we are looking at. Then we want to find those responsible for something, to blame God for all the injustice on Earth, to ask Him, «Why was He watching, allowing wars and tragedies.» When it comes to grief and sorrow, we turn to God, saying, «Oh, Lord, where have you been when we asked you for help?».

We, look at Heaven and what awaits us in life as if these are ordinary, not realizing that without some effort

we will never reach it. We believe the greatest value is an opportunity to live in happiness and harmony only at the present moment and after that comes what may. And we have no idea that life on Earth is just a pathetic copy of Heaven. It's the same thing as when coming for a visit and getting sight of a beautiful house, a neat lawn, trees, grass, admire the architecture and the richness of the house, knowing that it is even more beautiful inside. But having stayed in the yard, after seeing the house from the outside, we turn around and go away, saying to oneself: I've already seen everything, the courtyard is enough for me. That is how we feel about life in Heaven, having been in the yard (on the ground), we think that we have already seen everything, but we do not realize that what we see is just a small part of what awaits us in Heaven.

Life on Earth is good, it is interesting and fun, we have millions of parks, thousands of tourist attractions, beautiful buildings in the world, incredible landscapes, but these are just a shadow of Heaven.

Nicole went into the bus, in which every morning and every evening at a certain time she went from home to work and from her work to home. This process was repeated five times a week in the morning and evening - same route, same bus, same people. And, every day it was the same. Nicole went to the end of the bus and took out her phone to see the news of the day. But, that day she was so tired that she simply stood and stared at one point. It suddenly struck her that her life goes by every single moment and that she does not know

exactly what will happen to her tomorrow morning as she runs out of her house at 6:45 am to again catch the bus.

She began to see that her life was like a fog, and she sees only the repeating processes, but not life itself. She does not see the people who ride with her on the same route. She does not see the faces of people she meets on a daily basis. She does not see the streets she walks. She does not see anything.

Then Nicole came to the Summary that her whole life is a view through a dim glass on all that is happening around her. This is a lack of life itself.

Do you still think you do not live like our heroine? If you run, not seeing neither life, nor people who surround you, or what is happening around you, it is only an appearance of life, a view through a dim glass. But, this should not be our acquisition. Our goal is to see life on Earth around us in its entirety, to start living for those who are around.

Summary. *Love for God and our daily good deeds will bring us closer to the everyday achievement of Heaven.*

The Earth - is just a copy of Heaven, and living here we need to understand that somewhere there is a prototype on which all was originally created. It's the same thing as having a drawing of your house and seeing it at your desk across the murky, dim glass, not getting the full picture without knowing the exact dimensions. Not a single builder will undertake such a task to build a house haphazardly

because it is life threatening. But we do live life, not seeing what awaits us at the end of our lives, and at the same time, we are afraid of death, trying not to think about it. You may think that what you're trying not to think about will not get to you in your life. Death is inevitable, and it is an impartial fact.

We should not limit the understanding of God with our mind, thinking about what a beautiful Earth He has created, but then He allows human death and deprives people of all Earthly goods. Would you as a parent, having the opportunity to reward a son or daughter, pay the child with something that has no value, or doesn't look good? Yes, we are human beings and we are often guided by these thoughts «There is no place to put, and to throw out would be a pity, then I can give it away.» People may think so, but not God. His position is defined by the fact that we are His children, and we will inherit the best the Creator of the entire universe can give. Therefore, DEFEAT DEATH with your faith in the Father and that He will not give a stone to a child asking Him for bread.

So I would argue that life on Earth is the way of examination and trial in order to attain the beauty of life in Heaven, and, believe me, you will not be bored there.

THE EARTH AS A MIRAGE
Do not put off life for tomorrow

My friend opened his wife's drawer and took out a parcel wrapped in colored paper. It was not just any parcel, but a parcel with laundry. He threw out the wrapping and looked at the silk and lace.

— I bought this for her when we were in New York City for the first time, eight or nine years ago. She had never worn it. She wanted to save it for a special occasion. And now, I think the time has come.

He walked over to the bed and put the underwear on to the other things brought from the funeral house. His wife has passed away. He turned to me and said:

— Don't save anything for a special occasion; every day that you live is already a special occasion.

I still think about these words ... They have changed my life. Today, I read more and put things right. I sit down on the porch and enjoy the view, without paying attention to the weeds in the garden. I spend more time with my family and friends, and less at work. I have realized that life is a collection of experiences that must be valued...

Now I don't save things anymore. Every day I use our crystal glasses. If necessary, I put on my new jacket to go for a walk into town. Also, I use my favorite perfume when

~ 224 ~

I want to, rather than applying it only on holidays. Words like «once» or «one day» were banished from my vocabulary. If it's worth it, I want to see, hear and do something here and now.

I'm not sure what my friend's wife would do if she knew that she would not wake up the next day.. I think she would have called family and close friends. Maybe she would have called a couple of old friends to make peace or to apologize for the old quarrel. These small imperfect things would bother me if I knew that my days are numbered. I would be annoyed if I did not see the friends with whom I was supposed to get in touch with on one of those days.

Annoyed if I had not written a letter I wanted to write on one of those days. Annoyed if I haven't told my nearest and dearest how much I love them more.

Now I do not put off, I do not save anything that could bring joy and a smile into our lives. I tell myself that every day, as well as every minute, is special.

Everything in our life is special, and everything has its purpose – both life, and death. Death becomes your attainment when you see all its advantages when you love the truth and wish Heaven in your life. We must not lose daily chances to become the creator of history, because who knows if you will live tomorrow. The heroine of our story wanted to live «for later», but this did not happen, and her husband has shown us the image of her life on the example

of small clothes, which she kept for «the appropriate occasion». And how often do we live «for later», thinking: I will do this tomorrow and in the next month this ... But here comes a new day, and you again put off, defer all for tomorrow, which may or may not come.

The person who lives «for later». In death, will he carry out everything that he had to do? And what report will he give to the Creator of his life? Maybe, how skillfully he kept everything for «tomorrow»? It is appropriate to recall the parable of the talents that God has given each for multiplication in different quantities, and when he came to take them back, here is what he heard.

After a long absence, upon returning home, the master of those servants demanded their report. The one who has received the five talents came and brought another five talents, and approaching him said: «Master! Five talents you gave me; here are other five talents, I have gained beside them».

And the master said to him, 'Well done, good and faithful servant! You have been faithful over a little; I will set you over much. Enter into the joy of your master».

He also received two talents and said, «Master! Two talents you have given to me. Here are the other two talents I have gained».

And the master said to him, 'Well done, good and faithful servant! You have been faithful over a little; I will

set you over much. Enter into the joy of your master».

He who had received the one talent came and said, "Master, I knew you to be a hard man, reaping where you did not sow, and gathering where you did scatter no seeds; so, I was afraid, and I went and hid your talent in the Earth. Here' you have what is yours».

His master said to him: «A wicked and lazy servant! With your own mouth will I judge you; You knew that I reaped where I have not sown, and gathered where I scattered no seed; Therefore, You ought to have invested my money with the bankers, and at my coming I should have received mine with the interest. So, take the talent from him and give it to him who has the ten talents. For everyone who has more shall be given, and he will have abundance; But from the one who has not, even that will be taken away. And cast the worthless servant into the outer darkness (external); there will he be weeping and gnashing of teeth.»

I am not the one who said this; this is written in the Bible, the Book of Life. This story is an example for everyone to multiply all that you already have today. Today, to multiple life is to share it with others, to spend ourselves for others, to live and invest ourselves in those who are in need. If you sing well, become the best performer of the genre. If you are a successful businessman, become an example of quality and integrity for other businessmen, if you are a wise grandmother, pass all your wisdom to your grandchildren, and thereby you will multiply what you have.

Living «for tomorrow» and thinking that «tomorrow» you will start to multiply everything, you just adapt and agree with your conscience about «tomorrow». How do you think, living like this, will a person go to Heaven after his death? And where will he spend his eternity, do you think in Heaven? I would not argue that.

Summary. *By putting off for tomorrow, we are creating a mirage of our expectations and our actions.*

Mirage - a false vision, something apparent, illusory. Therefore, living «for later», with our own hands we are building our mirages in life, thinking, «As soon as I reach a certain period, I will start my life from the beginning; As soon as I earn my first million, I will start helping others; when I grow old, I will start to think about death, and what may come. « Who can hear your promises, except yourself?

That's what the expression «life is like a mirage.» means. Assuming that life on Earth is only a hint of life in Heaven, we can conclude that life on Earth is just a mirage.

We think we live. Tell me how you live, and what you live for, not just referring to the years of your life, not just talking about the number of children you brought up, but tell me, how many people have gained life and excelled because of you, because of your words and your actions? Name these thousand digits, because each of you has lived for more than a thousand days of your life. What is the point of your life? What rules your life? The circumstances

or difficulties that accumulate like a snowball, who controls the process, you? Tell me, honestly, inside your mind are you the man at the wheel, or do you simply accept what is going on around you?

We live or pretend that we live, telling ourselves: our life is unique, why should we think about what will happen in the future, why should we think about death, and about what will happen after it? But I want to draw your attention: we are only living on earth, a «copy» of Heaven. If you think about it, are we actually living? Is it life, when we lack the means of subsistence, when we cannot overcome the disease of the body, when we do not have the right to choose the kind of body we attain. Is it life when we are unhappy with everything that surrounds us, cold or too hot? Nevertheless, we hold on tenaciously to our belief that there is nothing better than life on Earth. **WE ARE TEMPORARY HOSTS ON EARTH.**

Summary. *To understand and appraise the importance of life in Heaven, we need to understand and compare it to life on Earth and to dream of a true and happy life in Heaven, do not be afraid to die, because death is just an opportunity to live fully.*

Life is like a mirage... And maybe, in fact, we are living an imaginary life and do not fully understand that this is just a platform for something more, that behind death there is actually a great victory of LIFE. Living on Earth is just a way of attaining a real life. Each of us must dream of eternity

in paradise, dream and do not limit your mind in this. It is here, on Earth, that we are limited financially, physically, and limited even with desires, in Heaven indeed everything will be possible!

Having dealt with the meaning of life on Earth, and how we can overcome the fear of death, in the next chapter we will talk about the advantages of Heaven, and how to live on Earth today, so we can attain Heaven tomorrow. But first, we need to solidify what we have identified in this chapter.

1. In order to understand the value of Heaven and attain knowledge about it, we should not put our opinion above the truth. All that we question without a personal analysis of the information, we immediately reject, and this leads to irreversible consequences.

2. Life on Earth is just a temporary shelter, so without thinking today about the future, we are going with the flow of circumstances and do not control the process of our future. Heaven is much real than the Earth, and if we do not understand this today, we will never be able to attain our tomorrow.

3. Living our life, we are creating a mirage of our future. Putting off life and decision-making for later, we never start living, but still we think things will happen one day. Mirage of life lies exactly in the fact that when we so quickly find ourselves in our «tomorrow», it will be too late to change anything.

GOLDEN TRUTHS

• Everything we do on Earth during the years of our life, will determine the place of our stay after the end of our physical life

• All that we have on Earth is like a mirror image of Heaven, but sin makes the Earth not to serve us in its fullness

• Doubt - is the information we reject, the facts we do not accept or even try to analyze

• Without efforts, we will never reach Heaven, with only wishing we cannot go to Heaven.

• Earth - it's just a dull image of Heaven

• If you run, noticing neither life, nor people who surround you, or what is happening around you, then it is only an appearance of life

• Life on Earth is a test in order to get the beauty of life in Heaven

• The man who lives «for later», dying, will not get his future in Heaven

• Living «for later», we are creating mirages in life, thinking: As soon as I reach a certain period, I will start my life from the beginning

• To understand and appreciate the importance and beauty of Heaven, we need to understand and compare it to life on Earth

TEST
«HOW NOT TO BUILD DUNGEONS IN THE AIR»

In each statement or question of the test, there should be only one answer. Next to each answer, in brackets, is a score. Your result of the test corresponds to the obtained amount of points.

1. What does the phrase «vanity of vanities» mean to you?
a) My fears (1)
b) Do not know (0)
c) My life (1)
d) A life without results (2)
e) Nothing is permanent in life (3)

2. Do you believe in luck, fortune?
a) Of course (1)
b) This what I'm counting on in my life (0)
c) Yes, and it often happens to me (1)
d) No, but I suppose that it can happen in my life (2)
e) I believe in the abilities and strength of developing my qualities (3)

3. Finding a purse on the street what will you do?

a) I will rejoice (1)

b) I will assure myself that it is good luck (0)

c) The most important to me, is so that no one notices, I found it (1)

d) I will accept it as a gift (2)

e) I will look for the contact information of the owner of the purse to return his belongings (3)

4. When deciding to start or change anything, do you often come around?

a) Yes, this does happen (1)

b) Yes, of course (0)

c) It is all the blame of circumstances (1)

d) It happens, but not often (2)

e) No, I am adhering to principles in my position (3)

5. Are you enjoying your life on Earth?

a) Of course (1)

b) It depends on (0)

c) I enjoy my life (1)

d) Yes, life is great, what could be better (2)

e) I enjoy when I see the results (3)

6. Can you imagine that life in Heaven will be millions of times more exciting than life on Earth?
a) I have not thought of this yet (1)
b) No, when will it be? (0)
c) It is difficult to believe so (1)
d) I concede such an idea (2)
e) I can and I do imagine a truly exciting life in Heaven (3)

RESULTS OF THE TEST

Less than 6 points. Life for you is just a self-centered existence, with the absence of believing in any capacity of the after life on Earth. Unfortunately, you think neither about the future of the Earth nor even about what will happen after your death. But by reading this book, you can accept all the beauty of Heaven and start living right from today in order to attain eternal life in Heaven.

7-12 points. You believe in the possibility of a life in Heaven, but this is not for certain for one simple reason: your doubts and the expectation that everything will go its way, will not bring you closer to the approving position. Do not build dungeons in the air, everything actually depends on you, on how you now live on Earth and multiplying your good deeds, or just waiting for Heaven.

13-18 points. Your life is in your hands. You are responsible for yourself and for what happens in your life. No miracle will change you, but you can become a miracle in the life of someone. Therefore, continue to draw a picture of their future in Heaven, knowing and accepting all the beauty of a true legacy for those who live for the people surrounding you.

PRACTICAL TASKS

1. What creates doubts in your mind about the existence of Heaven? Write at least three points.

2. How will you form an opinion about life in Heaven?

3. Which of your daily deeds will bring you closer to life in Heaven, what will you do today to inherit it?

4. Write three new solutions after reading this chapter of the book.

Recommended books of UNIVERSITY OF LIFE - «Values, we were deprived of.» Generate values inside your personality, and they will guide your actions. Due to the values, our actions will bring us closer to a full life for other people.

Chapter 7

BENEFITS
OF HEAVEN

Chapter 7
BENEFITS OF HEAVEN

In the previous chapter, we mentioned that we hear about chances of living in Heaven, but at the same time ignore everything that attracts us. We stated that the Earth is just an imitation of Heaven, and we need to understand that everything we see around us is just a hint of what we can have in Eternity.

Now, in this chapter, we will describe the advantages of life in Heaven and what is waiting for us, so that all our deeds during our Earthly life will be oriented towards the real life, the pale shade of which we have today.

You were running for so long from something that you have forgotten that you could run towards something.

Author unknown.

So, we always run from the thing that is going to get us eventually. The point is that the outcome should be acceptable to us. Death is inevitable, and WHAT IS COMING AFTER IT, depends on what we define as the most important in life. We will see Heaven for sure, though it is still a question whether we are going to spend eternity there.

The answer to this question is concealed in our everyday life on Earth. Therefore, every minute and every day I long for Heaven, and no matter what I do, I do it for the sake of eternity! So dear friend, let us continue. Let us draw a picture of Heaven, see the shades and a real life with all the benefits.

EVERYTHING IN THIS LIFE HAPPENS FOR A REASON

Once an atheist came to a wise man and started telling him, that he does not believe in God. He just could not believe in some "Creator" who created the Universe.

Few days later, the wise man came to the atheist and brought a marvelous painting. The atheist was stunned. He has never seen such a flawless painting before!

- What a remarkable piece of art. Tell me, who painted it? Who is the master?

- What do you mean who? No one! A canvas was lying on the floor under the shelf with paints. Accidentally, they fell from the shelf and spilled here is the result.

- Why are you making jokes? Laughed the atheist. That is impossible: great work, fine lines, the brush, palette of tones and shades. There is a deep concept behind this glorious painting.

The wise man smiled and said:

- Well, you cannot state that this small painting is a result of an accident, or it was executed without a preliminary plan of a Master. So you expect me to believe that our beautiful world with all mountains and forests, oceans and valleys, changes of seasons, fabulous sunsets and peaceful moon nights was created by accident, without the master plan of a Creator?

Someone made everything that we have in our world, someone drew the paintings, someone made the fancy clothes, wrote beautiful music. Nevertheless, who created the world? There cannot be a world without a Creator, there is no such place on Earth, which appeared just like that, or was anyone's life an accident? Everything is regular and proves to us that God was, is and will be and that Heaven is just as real as the Earth.

Here is what one student, who later became famous worldwide, has told about this.

A University Professor at a well-known institution of higher learning challenged his students with this question. «Did God create everything that exists?» A student bravely replied, «Yes he did!» «God created everything?» The professor asked. «Yes sir, he certainly did,» the student replied. The professor answered, «If God created everything; then God created evil. And, since evil exists, and according to the principle that our works define who we are, then we can

assume God is evil.» The student became quiet and did not answer the professor's hypothetical definition. The professor, quite pleased with himself, boasted to the students that he had proven once more that the Christian faith was a myth. Another student raised his hand and said, «May I ask you a question, professor?» «Of course», replied the professor. The student stood up and asked, «Professor, does cold exist?» «What kind of question is this? Of course, it exists. Have you never been cold?» The other students snickered at the young man's question. The young man replied, «In fact sir, cold does not exist. According to the laws of physics, what we consider cold is, in reality, the absence of heat. Everybody or object is susceptible to study when it has or transmits energy, and heat is what makes a body or matter have or transmit energy. Absolute zero (-460 F) is the total absence of heat, and all matter becomes inert and incapable of reaction at that temperature. Cold does not exist. We have created this word to describe how we feel if we have no heat.» The student continued, «Professor, does darkness exist?» The professor responded, «Of course it does.» The student replied, «Once again you are wrong sir, darkness does not exist either. Darkness is, in reality, the absence of light. The light we can study, but not darkness. In fact, we can use Newton's prism to break white light into many colors and study the various wavelengths of each color. You cannot measure darkness. A simple ray of light can break into a world of darkness and illuminate it. How can you know how dark a certain space is? You measure the amount of light present. Isn't this correct? Darkness is a term used by man to describe what happens when there is no light present .» Finally, the young man asked the professor,

«Sir, does evil exist?» Now uncertain, the professor responded, «Of course, as I have already said. We see it every day. It is in the daily examples of man's inhumanity to man. It is in the multitude of crime and violence everywhere in the world. These manifestations are nothing else but evil. To this, the student replied, «Evil does not exist, sir, or at least it does not exist unto itself. Evil is simply the absence of God. It is just like darkness and cold, a word that man has created to describe the absence of God. God did not create evil. Evil is the result of what happens when a man does not have God's love present in his heart. It's like the cold that comes when there is no heat or the darkness that comes when there is no light.» The professor sat down. The name of the young student was Albert Einstein. (22)

Do you still presume that anything in this life can happen by chance? There is no need to prove to you or to anyone else about Gods existence and his creations: Heaven and Earth. The only benefit of Earth over Heaven is that we can see it; at the same time, there is something more glorious and unreachable and that is Heaven. It does not mean that if we cannot see something it doesn't exist, we cannot see oxygen as well, but it is vital for life on Earth, we can't see the wind, but we are not used to saying that there is no wind, we cannot see a baby inside a mother's womb, but we know one hundred percent that he is there when we see a pregnant woman.

So we present you the story of a man who survived death and have seen Heaven.

I got sick. All of sudden, I felt as if I was sucked out of the room, but I didn't look back to see how I abandoned my physical body, as other people describe this. I felt that I was leaving the room and ascending with a fantastic speed. One more creature was standing next to me. I realized that it was a blonde angel.

Heaven is not that far. It seems that I didn't leave our galaxy. But, I am not an astronomer you know and can't be certain.

When I stepped out of the chariot, everything I saw around me was beautiful. I have always thought that when I will go to Heaven I will see only a city there, but the first thing I saw was paradise. Divine paradise is humongous, and it surrounds the Holy City. It looks as if you are on another planet. I was surrounded by marvelous blossoming valleys, lots of mountains and streaming water. I even saw snow though it was not cold. I was shocked.

One more clue about Heaven is that it has all four seasons that are on Earth. Winter and summer can be at the same time, though you will not feel cold, you will feel pleasure from what you see. It should be noted, that there is water, mountains, and blossoming valleys in Heaven, and it is so remarkable that the beauty of it is incomparable with what we can see during our Earthly life.

There are flowers in Heaven that I have never seen in my life, and flavors that I have never sensed before.

I have never seen colors with such tones and shades and they were red, green, purple, blue and yellow. Gold looked like gold though it was transparent as crystal.

I have always thought that everyone who goes to Heaven become an adult. But I have seen children there. I also spotted horses, dogs, and huge cats, which resembled lions.

You couldn't stomp the flowers! On our way, we stepped on the road laid out with flowers. The aroma and beauty of these flowers were incredible! I didn't want to step on them, but the angel said: "Go and step on them". So I did that. I was shocked when I saw that they were not breaking when you step on them, and then I realized that there is no death in Heaven. Every flower straightened up and as if turning to us when we were moving forward so we could see the beauty of it. There were no brown leaves on the plants. And, there was no dust in Heaven! Nothing can be damaged here, nothing is decomposing. There were no shadows in Heaven! (23)

The richness of color and beauty is waiting for us in Heaven. Everything that is in Heaven cannot die, there is no such notion like death because everything in Heaven is eternal including the aroma, a wealth of color, light, and flavor that you breathe in with every cell of your body. Is Heaven not marvelous, we can behold it through death? Fear of death has no power when you are aware of the benefits of being in Heaven. What does it mean to overcome the fear of death? It means to love life which comes after death and choose Heaven.

We cannot see life in Heaven, but it would be stupid to say that it does not exist. The only reason that the Earth exist is to prove that the Creator exists and He is in Heaven. Earth is just telling us about Heaven, as cold tells us that there is warmth. Everything is measured with Heaven but we devote more time to everything on Earth, it is important to have a cool Earth life, not to fall behind in our life at the same time neglecting all the value of life in Heaven.

There are no accidents in life, and if you think, that this book got to you by chance it is not so. It came to the right person who should read it. Even obstacles that we overcome in our life are not random their goal is to give us more than we have right now. I have heard lots of times that by overcoming the difficulties people have found God, believing in his power, embracing Him as their Lord and Savior. And, after that they found ways to overcome such difficulties like diseases, disappointment, addiction, loss, and found love, health, strength and faith in new and full life. This is the first stage of life with God. The aim of the second stage is to understand, that after life on Earth there is life in Heaven and we should long for it. **EVERYTHING WE DO ON EARTH WE DO TO HAVE HEAVEN IN OUR LIFE.**

YOU BREATH WITH LOVE.

Heaven is real and unbelievably beautiful. No stories of people whom God allowed to see Heaven is accidental: they have seen it and they have shared all they felt and saw. So, we ought to live our lives the way we should and not the way we want. This is necessary in order to overcome the fear of death and start to live for Eternity in paradise after death.

So, Heaven gives us the chance to live with love. Why love? Because there is no other pure feeling as love. Not the kind of love when you are waiting for another, not the kind of love when you get what you desire, but that true love that fills your heart with warm, care, compassion, and joy. All these feeling are working in one direction, and become valuable for someone. Help someone today, bring joy to your surroundings, and carry love to the world.

On Earth most people only feel love to people close to them; their parents, children, wives, and husbands. God shows us with the help of these relationships what love means. How can you transfuse feelings between two people, which thoughts are only about upcoming meetings? After the birth of a child, the mother experiences feelings after passing through the birth pangs and finally seeing her child. Love for a child is passed through joy, concern, laughter, and just looking at the baby. These things are felt with every fiber of our being. The feeling of love loses

its power here on Earth, because of frustration, resentment, uncertainty, and weakness. When loved ones fall short of our expectations. This weakens the love, and love finally loses its power, but this only happens on Earth; in Heaven, that will never happen. It's simple: in eternity, there're no such feelings as resentment, pain, frustration, uncertainty, and helplessness. All that is in Heaven radiates just one feeling; perfect love.

One man who survived cardiac arrest, says that he went through the tunnel, into the bright light, beautiful, golden, coming from an unknown source. It was everywhere, occupied all the surrounding space.

Then the music started, and the man thought that he was among the trees, streams, and mountains. But, it turned out that he was wrong, nothing similar was there. But, there was a sense of people's presence. He did not see them, he just knew they were close. He was filled with a sense of perfect peace, love, and satisfaction; he has become a part of that love.

Becoming a part of love is what Heaven means, that's what it means to feel love with all of your body and mind, and not just feeling it, but making it become a part of you.

Remember the best feeling you had obtained from love. For example, you are hugging someone, you feel it all over, enjoying the hug, receiving warmth, tenderness, protection, confidence in the fact that you are not alone.

Now multiply those feelings by a hundred billion times. Do you think it will be a momentary feeling? No! But, still this feeling ends when you stop strengthening it, but in Heaven, this feeling will last forever. What we are experiencing on Earth is just a bit of fullness, it is the same as 0.00000000001 from 100.

For example, you are told that you have a thousand dollars, but you only get one cent. Will you enjoy it, knowing there is a thousand dollars for you somewhere? Will you rejoice in only a vestige part? This comparison now moves on to the feeling of love.

Here on Earth, we have only an echo of love, just a small part of it. On Earth, we need to have a husband or wife in order to at least roughly understand what love is. And, in Heaven, there is no need for this, because every cell in our body receives the love of all that surrounds us. But living here on Earth, because of the fear of losing love, we fear death. We are afraid that we won't be loved or that we cannot love anymore. This is a myth. Love is like the air in Heaven, this is everything all the inhabitants of Heaven live upon. Even the flowers will tell you about love, your body will tell you about love, the wind will carry the words of love across Heaven.

Love is everywhere, and everything breathes love in Heaven. Imagine you're walking down the street and get love from the road; you see the trees, and they give you love, feelings escalate from everything that surrounds you

in Heaven. On Earth, we need air to live. Well, in Heaven, we do not need air; we need love, which fills the whole of Heaven.

Family ties only try to convey to people what kinship is so that we understand what acceptance is, what it means to love, to be close to each person. These relationships are needed on Earth to open up a little understanding of what love is and how it can be in Heaven. Love speaks at various levels of feelings and organs of the body. We can fall in love, experience the passion, respect, and patriotism in order to understand different levels of love, and we experience it in different ways and with different parts of the body. For example, sex is a sensual pleasure, that is experienced within, enjoying the touch from the outside.

So, to live and breathe love in Heaven is to feel it, not only by a single sense organ but every bit of its internal and external content. Women for example, make more use of their organ of hearing, they like to listen to words of love and tenderness. Men on the other hand, are moved by what they see. Now imagine that you are saturated with everything, even your nails are saturated with what surrounds them, our hair enjoys the grass, the road, with all that surrounds us. Isn't it a wonderful feeling of love that we will experience to the fullest in Heaven?

Love is the only source of existence in Heaven, which allows you to enjoy all the beauty of life.

Moreover, in Heaven love is equal to all that surrounds you, and to all people who are there. In Heaven, there is no need to love someone more or someone less. Love simply is, and you feel it from everything and from everyone around you. Same thing with pleasure. If say you eat ice cream on Earth, or your favorite cake and enjoy it only through your taste buds, in Heaven you will also experience this delight with your eyes and ears.

Summary. *There's no temporary pleasure in Heaven, all in Heaven is perfect love and enjoyment of anything that surrounds us.*

Do you want to conquer the fear of death then start loving people, begin to live for the love of people, and God, and then you will not only overcome the fear of death but also gain Heaven as a reward of your life.

Heaven is neither high nor low, neither right nor left, the sky is straight to the middle of the chest of the man who has faith.

Salvador Dali, Spanish painter

Quite interesting words of one of the most extraordinary artists of the 20th century. I suggest talking a little bit about him and summing up that Heaven is the image each of us draw during our life on Earth to know what to strive for daily.

Salvador Dali; *He was hated and admired. He was called the most controversial artist of the 20th century. Some considered him a genius, others crazy. People spend time and effort trying to penetrate the mystery of Salvador Dali, they were sure he has a secret.*

He created about 2000 painting. These paintings could not cease to amaze. They were way beyond, another reality, unusual images. In these paintings, the elephants walked on bird legs and women with heads of flowers, beckoning somewhere illusory door, and a ghost carriage rolled into the fog. Salvador Dali was pleased about all the talk around his paintings and strongly encouraged the interest to his persona. You can argue whether he is a genius as a painter, but one thing is certain: he was a genius of self-promotion.

In 1940, he went to America. His fame in the US began with the fact that he broke the window of a luxury shop «Tiffany», throwing a stone at the glass. Then he offered his services to the owner of the store for the new window dressing. He agreed. The artist set a bath of red wine and sat a beauty with an emerald ring on his finger in it. People crowded into the store ... In America Dalí worked as a goldsmith, designer, illustrator, painter, photographer, portraits; he published a newspaper «Dali News.» His name has become a powerful brand. There were tights and perfumes «by Dali.» Fragments of his paintings could be seen on furniture sets and ties. He became a multimillionaire. The Americans recognized him as a genius.

«The Rider Named Death» the title of one of his paintings. As any intelligent person, he thought about life and death. He knew that everything in this world is relative. Nothing is perfect, permanent, eternal in this material, and inconsistent world. In place of the classical comes avant-garde, some ideas displace other, war replaces peace, and life succeeds death. You can live your life like no one else, but the end is the same for everyone.

«I obscenely love life», confessed the artist. Inability to live forever he perceived as a tragedy.

«Well, will humankind go to space, and what? What is space were you not given eternity? »

One of his favorite images the soft watches, melting time. Dali did not want to be forgotten with time. And, then he decided to create the illusion of eternity. Having invested all his money, he built a theater in Figures, Dali Museum the building of Baroque architecture, filled it with his paintings and sculptures, and buried himself in the museum previously embalmed. There in this strange building exterior decorated with huge white eggs, he spent his last years. They were sad. Antidepressants, which his wife Gala gave him undermined his health. Gala's death broke him completely. Dali fell ill. He was driven in a chair and fed through a tube. He was totally dependent on other people. He could not speak, constantly crying and uttered animal sounds for hours. He wanted to paint, but could not hold a brush.

It so happened that at that time he was alone. There was no one next to him. His father had died, he had long ceased communication with his sister, and he had no children, no friends as well. And, the blame for this was on Dali himself, who, according to people who knew him, acted too selfish. The pain rips all the masks. Even the most incorrigible liars stop pretending if suffering. He was not pretending. A man who spent his entire life in the pleasure endured all of this very seriously. He tormented and tortured others. He's throwing plates at his sitters, tormented them with their whims. And, wanted to see no one. He did not want outsiders to see him the way he was.

He died at eighty-five, holding the hand of an old servant Arthur Kaminadu. His last words were: «I want to go home.» Three days before death, Salvador Dali invited the parish priest with the Blessed Sacrament. He Confessed and took communion. It is said that in a fit of remorse, he exclaimed: «My God! How you allow me ...»

*His last painting «**The Swallow's Tail**» is simple, like a child's drawing. Several regular lines and careless zigzag violate all symmetry. Like all his life in one stroke. What's on it is not even a tail; it is a trace of a passing swallow tail, the invisible track, quickly melting into the air ... (24)*

Salvador Dali a millionaire, a man who had it all. He was loved by millions, his legacy is still significant, and he left a mark in the history of modern painting. But it did not make him happy, made it impossible to extend the days

of his life in joy, fame and money did not make him immortal and happy, but the pain of loss and the pain of death left him all alone. As much as he wanted to live, death was imminent, the body failed him in old age, and it was directed against him. This is the inevitability of anyone who dies in the weakness of the body.

Summary. *We believe that life, even in the old, frail body a much better life in the fullness of joy, love, and perfection.* We did not assess the possibility of death, because it is much easier to hold on to what we already have, than not knowing what will happen after we die.

Dear reader, do not chase the illusion of the world, do not build castles in the sand, thinking that someone or something will make you happy, apart from God and His love. We are all just sounding brass. We can talk about Heaven, but the truth is that we do not come close to the knowledge of Heaven and of God himself, and will not be able to gain it all in this life on Earth.

Summary. *Everything new in our life begins with love.*

A person can make new discoveries out of love for the cause, for the people to whom this discovery will help. Children should be born out of love too, but on Earth sometimes our love to someone may be distorted due to our selfishness. Love in Heaven is perfect because nothing can be without love, like the Earth itself would not exist if God didn't love the world.

AN OPPORTUNITY TO BE ANYTHING YOU WANT

Let's continue our journey to Heaven. When a child is born, he does not choose the parents, the place of birth, much less the gender. Being born, we are limited by the terms of our birth, our body, and the meager set of capabilities that we have. I was born in Africa, for example, and some of you in Europe. We are children of two different continents, and we did not choose it. Parents are just able to provide for the children where to live. But as for Heaven: we have the opportunity to make a choice of Heaven, or to accept and live for an eternal Hell.

In Heaven there are no limits, everything is possible for those who live there. For example, you are a fair complexioned woman living in the northern part of Russia, but in Heaven, you can be whom you want, without restrictions. Want to become a black person it is not a problem, want to be a Chinese woman, it is also possible. All these happen at the level of the mind. Yes, it may seem strange and unrealistic, and may not look feasible. For humans yes, this is not feasible, but for God nothing is impossible. God is not limited by our mind and our perception of opportunities. For example, what can you do in your life today? Just what you saw or just what you are allowed to see by yourself in your mind, but God sees everything and sees its fullness, not fragments and pieces. If you see a person, you are focusing on how they are dressed and how they speak, at best. But God, sees every thought of

this person, the assumptions of the heart and God knows even what the person had not thought about yet.

Don Piper had an accident on 18 January 1989. He was declared dead. Then Piper returned to life. During this time, he managed to make an unforgettable journey to another world.

At the moment of death, Piper felt that he was flying through a long dark tunnel. Suddenly, he was covered with a very bright light, it was indescribable. He recalled that he felt a vibrating pleasure. Looking around, he saw a very beautiful gateway to Heaven and a group of people in front of them. It turned out that all of these people were his friends who died during his lifetime. They were very happy to meet him with smiles. There were so many of them and they were very happy. The whole picture was filled with the most vivid colors, warm light, and it was enjoying the beauty, unprecedented sensation. Piper felt like everybody loved him and he soaked up this love, enjoying the scene. The surrounding people were beautiful, without wrinkles and signs of aging, so they looked how he remembered them in a lifetime.

The gates of Heaven shone brighter than the light around them. Literally, everything was shining, so that it was difficult to describe. With the whole group, they went ahead. Beyond the gate, was also a bright light. That lights that were initially emanating from the greetings was gradually pale in comparison with that light. The farther they moved, the lighter it became. Then there was music,

very pleasant and beautiful music, and it was not stopping. It filled his heart and soul. The rustle of angel wings was heard and songs of praise in honor of God. Piper felt that he was back at home, he did not want to leave that place. (25)

The incredible light of Heaven, an incredible feeling of love, and acceptance are mentioned again. Don saw the people he loved in a perfect body without sickness nor the effects of old age. Heaven is life; love is what fills the life of someone who would be there. And, most importantly, we think that the Earth is an advantage, but it's only because we do not know the advantages of Heaven. Even this person did not want to go back to all the «advantages» of the Earth, and his desire was to exchange all that he had in life with the ability to stay and live in Heaven. And, we think how it can be, because it is bad not to see all the relatives and people close to us. Yes, this time, meetings are incomparable with advantages of living in eternity, with the ability to stay in the infinite love with all those who have lived on earth before or passed away.

Once on the Earth, we are limited in our mind, then going to Heaven, where everything is done at the level of a thought, we will not have any restrictions. Everything you want will become dependent on your desires and your thoughts. But, do not dream about it in the flesh now in your mercantile requirements. Previously, we have said that all in Heaven is love and thoughts will be directed to it. There will be no selfishness, jealousy and disappointment

in Heaven everything will be done in love and pleasure. Therefore, while living on Earth today, we should see the opportunities around us to serve in order to become a response to people, in order to solve the problems of the society, and not live in the little world of our desires.

The Route to Heaven

The trolleybus was driving on its regular route. People were coming out and going in. For the last stop on the train were two women and a small, poorly dressed boy with large and very sad eyes. One woman came out in the last stop. The conductor was thinking that the boy was with her and called out:

— Did you forget your baby?

— What baby? The homeless boy cannot be my son - she said with disgust.

— Who are your parents, boy? Are you lost? - The conductor asked sympathetically.

— Boy? I'm nobody. And, I am alone.

— A child cannot be nobody's. Where is your mother? Are you lost?

— My mother has gone to Heaven. I also want to go there. Do you know what trolley goes to Heaven?

— *There is no such route. And, it is not easy to get there.*

— *But, I want to see my mom ... Is there nothing I can do to reach Heaven?*

Then another younger woman came to the boy, gave him a hug, and gently pressed to her chest.

— *What's your name, son?*

— *Actually, I am Michael. But, I am called 57 now.*

— *?*

— *I live in an orphanage. There are a lot of us. And, nobody has a mom. The teacher cannot remember all the names and calls us by numbers.*

— *Is it hard for you, baby?*

— *Nobody loves me. Mom always kissed me. She read me a bedtime story and sang a lullaby. And, we prayed together. I want to see my mother. She left and never returned. Were you in Heaven?*

— *Not yet, sweety. But, I know how to get there. You will not find the way by yourself. Do you want me to take you to my home? We will live together, and wait for Christ. He can lead us to Heaven, where your mother is living right now.*

The boy's eyes shone with hope. He clung to the good woman, as to his mother, and she gently stroked his head and smiled.

At the last stop, they got out. The conductor with the driver looked long after them. One of them said:

— The «Heaven» stop is not marked on our route. But still, I think it is on this line.

God lives where love lives. Where God is, Is close to Heaven.

Even in this story, you can see how an ordinary woman changed the life of a child who needed love by the way she related to him. She has made a choice to become a mother to the boy. She also had the choice to move on and not notice, or hear the boy. We even have a choice on Earth to decide whom we want to be.

Summary. *If you want to be a «blind businessman» just live for yourself, want to be a "grumpy wife" then do not notice the needs of the husband, and want to be "unfulfilled individual" just live in your pleasure.*

Then, it is not necessary to live in the hope that after death, Heaven will be your reality. **IT IS EASY TO WIN THE FEAR OF DEATH**, we just need to stop living for ourselves and know that we have done everything we can to people we know.

In order to choose our future, there is a today that will determine our future in Heaven; you have the choice to become someone, and this «someone» can remain simply an impersonal word, or may be the position of the individual. The choice on Earth is limited by our ability to think and reflect, but the choice to be whom we want has no limitation in Heaven, as the Creator of Heaven and Earth is infinite in His possibilities. And, Heaven will not have restrictions to anyone who will let the Lord be seen in their lives and in their actions. Here's what the Bible says about this: «Rejoice and be glad because great is your reward in Heaven» (Matthew 5:12).

God tells us that we should rejoice, have fun despite what is going on in our life today, and aspire to receive great rewards in Heaven. Because the difficulties and the problems on the Earth are temporary. Life in Heaven is eternal, and cannot be numbered in time or space.

NO LIMITATIONS TO THE BODY AND TO THE MIND

"There are no limitations to the mind except those that we acknowledge."

Napoleon Hill

There are no limitations to the mind, but we often create it with our inner feelings, fears, unbelief, and total insecurity. There is nothing like that in Heaven, there is no such thing as a lack of confidence, low self-esteem or impotence. Just because we see a picture of the real world, lawlessness, see ourselves in different situations, take the words of others at our expense, we are limited. In Heaven, even your body will tell you words of love and you will feel them as power and love, you cannot be limited.

On Earth, we are concerned with our desires, judgments emanating from other people, the temptations around us, but the one who can pass through it and remain faithful to God, will be able to live in joy and perfection in Heaven. That's what God's Word says: « Blessed is the one who perseveres under trial because, having stood the test, that person will receive the crown of life that the Lord has promised to those who love him.» (James 1:12). The crown of life is a life in Heaven; it is an opportunity to live forever in Paradise, without pain, humiliation, temptation, and death. But as we see, only the one who will be able to overcome the temptations of the world, while remaining faithful to God until his death, to the last breath of his life on Earth will get it. We are afraid to die, not knowing that the only way to overcome the fear of death is living right while on Earth.

What limits our mind, what doesn't allow us to see the beauty of Heaven, while on Earth? You can say that we are not given this or that. Thinking that there are special

people it was made for, but today the only restriction in your life is you.

Summary. *You can be told, a lot about Heaven and its advantages, but without a picture in our head, not knowing the way of life after death, we will not be able to live in Heaven.*

A couple of centuries ago, looking at the white color, people have seen white. But, now most of us know that the white color contains a lot more colors than we can see with our own eyes.

The Connection between the rainbow and color of the body was discovered only in the remarkable study by Isaac Newton (1642-1727) in the middle of the 17th century. Newton refracted white light with a prism, resolving it into its component colors: red, orange, yellow, green, blue and violet. Newton came to the Summary that there are plain colors that are not laid out on the spectrum when passing through the lens, and complex, representing an aggregate (mixture) is simple. Newton's second discovery was that the white color is the set of simple colors. The rainbow is a color pattern of white. (26)

We see white color while others could see other colors in it, such as blue, red, yellow, and so on. What does this mean? Not everything we see has a look and shape as it seems to view; behind that form, color or space may be a spectrum of life.

Summary. *Considering the question of death, we should not see the end, but the beginning of true life.*

Seeing Heaven, we only see what we allow ourselves to imagine because of our perception. Do you see the fear of death, and then you imagine it. Do you think that after death you'll go away forever into the unknown? In case you want to see life, start to imagine all the advantages of Heaven where there is no death, jealousy, and there is only life and love that fills every cell of your body, understanding, and awareness. Here is what psychologists are saying about this.

The restrictions created in the mind lead people to the beings created for light and joyful life are compelled to live in the world where there is suffering, wars, violence, and injustice. Living conditions and an environment put certain restrictions in the programming of a person.

Restrictions frame is created by the imagination. If you'll pay attention to what's happening inside, you can notice that your mind is imagining all the restrictions. The main restriction of the mind is its ideas of itself and the world around which it builds from the wrong concepts, belief, and stereotypes. Life according to the programs put in our subconsciousness and the ability of the mind to work only in their limits reminds us of a game with certain conditions and rules.

Mind, wandering in time and space, constantly imagines some events. Being involved in actions of the mind and being

identified with your imagination, you become the participant of the events imagined by it. But, all rules and all games exist only in your mind. And, all your life completely depends on that, how attentively and consciously you approach formation of the programming, establishing game rules under the name «your life». (27)

As we see, everything depends on us and if we start drawing the picture of Heaven today, to form the programming of life on Earth so that the only ultimate goal of life will be Heaven, just believe, and all our words and actions will be directed on living for Heaven. As you will develop your imagination, such impulses it will give will affect your daily reactions, and you will only live for Heaven.

For example, if you imagine how you will help other people, to draw images of people who need your help, you won't neglect those people in real life; you will begin to help them, despite fatigue or business. You will start acting so in life, and you will be surprised that now you aren't indifferent and careful. In other words, everything that you imagined transformed into real acts. But, moreover, helping another, you will see how you change your life situations.

We are very limited on Earth with our bodies, and every year, especially after fifty years, we start losing our strength. No matter how hard we try we are still getting old. There are always seasons, whether we want them or not. The winter will always be after fall, but not after summer.

Even in our twenties we understand that time isn't simply going, it flies and by 25 years women will begin to see the first wrinkle on the face, which specifies that youthfulness is now been replaced by maturity, and further along the line, old age comes. And, despite an era of super technologies in medicine, including the cosmetic surgeries, none will hinder death, it will still occur.

It is possible to get into the car and drive at a speed of 150-200 kilometers per hour. It is possible, but everything depends on the type of car you are driving: if it is an old «Zhiguli», you won't be able to go at the speed you want. But, if it is a brand new model of «Mercedes», I am sure it can move very fast.

As we live on in life, the body limits us, therefore, we should maximize each day living in such a way that we come closer to a life in Heaven, reaping its advantages. We must not live for ourselves, living for self will eventually lead to disappointments.

In Heaven, our body won't wear out, rather, it will have a perfect form. This best state is unattainable during our lifetime on Earth. Earlier, I said that the body will be excellent and perfect not only in beauty but also by the opportunities which won't be limited only to what we have on Earth. . Because on Earth, our body is influenced by both an image of food, and the influence of our habitat; illness and physical work included. But there won't be anything like that in Heaven where the body is perfect. Your

body won't have wounds, it will be perfect. In Heaven, there is no headache or waist pain, there is no such term as pain which we endure here on the Earth.

Jeff is a young man at the prime of his life. Judging by appearance, he is a self-assured and well-groomed man who looks as a youth in his forties. His way of life speaks of how he cares for his health; he doesn't drink, doesn't smoke, and is mindful of what he eats. But periodically he is absent from work for some weeks. This happens for one reason he can't get up from bed because of his back pain.

As a young and ambitious guy, he wanted to enjoy life, therefore in his off time he had a side job in construction. Not an easy work to carry cement bags, to mix tons of cement grouts every day for two months of summer. The body broke down due to this strenuous work and one morning Jeff got out of bed knowing that something wasn't right with his body. But despite it, he ran to work. In the evening, he had an appointment with his future wife Delia. Having worked till the evening, Jeff understood that the situation was grave but didn't miss the date. After consulting with the doctor, it showed that Jeff had a vertebral hernia.

After twenty years, the situation with his health detoriated: Jeff thought that his young body will cope with the problem and that it isn't so dangerous and continued to live as he lived. But today in his forties, he can't handle this anymore, not because he lifts weights, no, he works at the office. But the slightest stress aggravates his state and has made him to be bedridden.

Very few people know what's going on inside a healthy looking body.

Externally, all people are beautiful, but nobody knows their pain nor their disappointments. Our life becomes limited because of symptoms of various diseases and simply imaginary shortcomings of our body. Someone looks and thinks they are fat and doesn't want to live, dreaming of being thin, someone does not want to be lean, but wants to put on some weight. We see people dissatisfied with their body and there are lots of people with this problem. But in Heaven, our life and pleasure will not depend on a body because it's perfect. Everything in Heaven will reflect only love, all that surrounds us will reflect love. You will see beauty in yourself, imagine how happy you will be seeing your hands, your nose, your feet, and even your fingers, this sight will bring you only joy and inexpressible feeling of delight.

Summary. *In Heaven, everything radiates with joy and life, and the body is no exception.*

I do not know about you, but I live for Heaven. It is my goal to live not for the sake of a beautiful body, but to live my life without the world's limitation in order to be accepted in Heaven. So I enjoy thinking about Heaven, I see it clearly and concisely in my mind, I see myself in Heaven and wait for my arrival to life which will begin in Heaven.

It's good to dream, and it is necessary to have a desire, but what are our dreams without action? It's just a desire without fulfillment in reality. Therefore, in the next chapter, we'll talk about how to live today, to approach the reality of life in Heaven. But first, read the summary of this chapter.

1. Still believe in coincidence? Coincidence is for those who agree to participate in life as observers, they see life as an accident. There are no accidents in the world and in human life, every happening is the idea of the One who created the world and gave us the opportunity to be born. If your life is the plan of the Creator, so He has entrusted you to become a part of life, not only on Earth; He expects that you will inherit Heaven.

2. In Heaven, there is one vital advantage, love. Love is the foundation, the essence of Heaven. There are no other personal requirements or expectations in Heaven. Everyone is engulfed and surrounded with love; and the desire to give and receive that love.

3. Do not restrict the notion of eternity only by your mind. Heaven is the source of all that we have on the Earth. Inventions made by people on Earth shows how majestic God has made Heaven to be. If today you can make a call just by pressing one button, it is only a small capacity of Heaven that God has entrusted to men on Earth, showing the power of His limitlessness.

4. In Heaven, there are no restrictions of the body or mind. Our Earthly limitations of the mind depend on our perception of everything that surrounds us. Seeing Heaven, we can afford to see the clouds, or the color of the clouds, or imagine a full, interesting life with unlimited possibilities. It all depends on what we allow ourselves to see behind the normal words that we use in everyday life or the end of life.

GOLDEN TRUTH

• The goal of this subject is to show us today that God is, was and will be, and that Heaven is so real as what we see here on Earth

• Earth's only advantage is that it mirrors Heaven. There is something much grandeur in Heaven

• Everything we do on Earth serves only to help us achieve Heaven

• Heaven is an opportunity to live with love

• In Heaven, there are no such feelings as resentment, pain, frustration, uncertainty, and helplessness. Love is the only feeling in Heaven

• On Earth, we need air to live, but in Heaven, love fills the whole place

• There are no limits in Heaven, everything is possible over there

• On Earth, we are limited in our mind, but in Heaven, where everything is done at the level of thought, we will not have any restrictions

• Choices on Earth are limited by our ability to think and reason while the choice to be who you want, in Heaven has no restrictions, as the creator of Heaven and Earth is infinite in his possibilities

• On Earth, we are pinned down by our desires, judgments emanating from other people and also the temptations around us. But the one who can pass through it and remain faithful to God will be able to live in joy and perfection in Heaven

• In Heaven, our body will not wear out. It would be in perfect shape, the best condition, which is unattainable for us while living on Earth

TEST
"APPROACH
OF THE HEAVEN"

In each statement or question of the test, there should be only one answer. Next to each answer, in brackets, is a score. Your result of the test corresponds to the obtained amount of points.

1. How do you feel about life on Earth?
a) Currently living (1)
b) As each day brings (0)
c) Live for new achievements (2)
d) As an opportunity to live qualitatively for the future (3)

2. Do you see a future in heaven?
a) Don't even know (1)
b) What is Heaven, I don't see it on Earth (0)
c) It is possible to try (1)
d) Yes, I imagine it (2)
d) I see and I know that life will begin in Heaven (3)

3. What is love?
a) Passion (1)
b) Emotions and nothing more (0)
c) Family, children (1)
d) Acceptance of other people (2)
e) Serving others (3)

4. Why do you feel pain in your body?
a) Because I do not take good care of it (1)
b) I was a weak child since childhood (0)
c) It is not possible to be treated (1)
d) I'm old, the pain reminds me about it (2)
e) I feel it because my body limits me (3)

5. Heaven - it is real! Could this be your motto?
a) Yes, when I'm old (1)
b) No, I am convinced of my submissions (0)
c) In fact, as I see it over me every day (1)
d) Yes, it can (2)
e) This is my way of life today (3)

RESULTS
OF THE TEST

Less than 5 points. You live an ordinary life, not wanting to think beyond what you see. Heaven for you is an illusion that you have selected for your stay on Earth. You should not limit your mind, allow yourself see a bit more than usual, and Heaven will be your reality.

6-9 points. You seek to know Heaven, but the limitations of your mind do not allow you that due to the lack of information on Heaven. Start reading this book not just as a set of letters. See the image of Heaven in your mind and think about it while reading this book.

10-15 points. You see the clarity of Heaven in the future today. Life for you - is an opportunity to approach Heaven through actions and deeds. Reading this book makes your opinion about Heaven more clearly, this will help you tell other people about Heaven.

PRACTICAL
TASKS

1. Who made your life?

2. What qualities help you in dealing with people? What qualities prevent you from dealing with people, how can you get rid of them?

3. What would you like to be, where will you want to live and which things will you like to do? Dream to the maximum today.

Recommended books from the UNIVERSITY OF LIFE - «Who will come to your funeral?» Realizing that life is an opportunity of a moment, we can change our attitude to both life and to daily actions and words.

Chapter 8

THE MEANING OF
LIFE
ON EARTH IS TO
LIVE
FOR HEAVEN

Chapter 8
THE MEANING OF LIFE
ON EARTH IS TO LIVE FOR HEAVEN

In the previous chapters, we have learned about death and its acquisition. How beautiful Heaven is, the meaning of love, what it means to live a life of love when either our body or the mind is not limited to our usual understanding. Next, we will talk about life on Earth, how to overcome the fear of death and to live the life that would bring us closer to Heaven. After all, you can just live, and at the end of your years discover the evidence that Heaven exists, but it is already impossible to change anything, there is no turning back, you can't be wise after death.

Many of us probably already have heard this phrase. The meaning is very deep:

"The most precious thing a man has is life. He only lives once and should live it so that he wouldn't be sorry for the wasted years, that he did not feel the shame of his sneaky and petty past and when dying, he could say: I spent all of my life and made a real effort to do the most important thing in the world: I struggled for the liberation of humanity. We must hurry to live. After all, some illness or some tragic accident can interrupt it."

"How the Steel Was Tempered" N. A. Ostrovsky

We have got one life so we have the right to choose how to live it, carelessly or not, we can draw a plan for our life on Earth and life after death.

Summary. *Live your life the way that your affairs, actions, and words, even after the sudden tragic end of life on Earth, can acquire a life in Heaven.*

YOUR LABOR ON EARTH DETERMINES YOUR ETERNAL DESTINATION.

"We never keep to the present. We recall the past; we anticipate the future as if we found it too slow in coming and were trying to hurry it up, or we recall the past as if to say its too rapid flight. We are so unwise that we wander about in times that do not belong to us and do not think of the only one that does; so vain that we dream of times that are not and blindly flee the only one that is."

Blaise Pascal
Philosopher, inventor, writer

Do we live in the present or speed up events? One day, we will not have time to live another day and we may regret that we didn't live our life to the fullest. We are really like the foolish, wondering about life, and kind of creatures, who think: «That this is only the beginning!» and at the same time don't realize that it is the time we neglect. The fear of death increases when we live aimless lives

lives and when running out of time we realize that we lived a worthless ordinary life. The only thing that is fair, whether you are a businessman or a young student – is time, that each of us has 24 hours a day. But how do you spend your time? At the computer, on a telephone conversation with your friends, working, aimlessly hanging out at the local shops. How do you spend your time? How do you spend your 24 hours? It's not so little a time as much as 24 hours, because someone only lived a couple of hours today, someone even a couple of minutes, and there are those for whom time has already expired.

Summary. *The only thing worth worrying about is every minute of our life. After all, who knows, maybe it is the only thing we have today.*

What or who determines the time we spend on Earth? Whatever you do today and how you spend your 24 hours of life is only your choice, but you must understand that it is the result of your life that will determine whether you will live after death in Heaven or spend eternity in Hell. Remember, the result of life is not the number of years you lived, everyone has their own and it depends on how you live your life today. The result of life is your current 24 hours which began and will end this day.

I want to recall one proverb that clearly indicates our attitude towards Heaven: **"Pray as though everything depends on God. Work as though everything depends on you."** You ask: "How does this relate to Heaven?" It's simple

everything we did during life will determine where we will spend eternity; In Heaven or Hell?

Whom are you working for today? You might think that this is a strange question, but still: for whom? If you hurry to work in the morning and rush home in the evening not to miss the news on your favorite channel then you live for yourself and family. And that's not bad, but do you see in your life anything not only needs and desires of your family? We should understand that we will be responsible before God for our life on Earth. What would you say to Him? That you were so busy with yourself and benefits for your family that you didn't see anything or anyone around? But, this doesn't justify you. One day you will realize with bitterness that you have never lived your life, it has passed you by. The result of this life will disappoint you. Even today we can say what happens to those people after they die, they spend eternity in Hell. Common sense seems to tell us: no one was killed and nothing was stolen by us, but the outcome is only one for those who didn't accept God into their life and didn't devote themselves to one another.

No wonder the following words were written in the Bible: *"For if you love those who love you, what reward do you have?"(Matthew 5:46)* These words teach us that family is given to us, not in order to live our life for them but to be able to understand what love is. Our life should not be devoted to these people, we need to understand that living the life for only those we love may hurt them and ourselves. What may happen if we devote ourselves only to our family?

1. Indifference. Yes, we do love our children, parents, spouses. That now concludes the list. It's simple: the one who lives only for this unit of society, becomes indifferent to what is going on and the main point for him is that everything is okay at home. Indifference is the virus when a society is incapable of empathy, love and help for those who are in need.

2. "Self - comes first." This proverb tells us that for some of us, the well-being of our family we value more than principles or positions. This means that if the issue is related to honor or justice such people will ignore all of these principles only to justify their loved ones. They would take their principles to the back seat as long as their relatives are all right. This leads to lawlessness, frauds, thefts, profitable connections and consumer attitudes towards life.

3. Life is like an empty well. When people live only for themselves they only draw and use their energy, they are not filled by others with gratitude, love and care about someone. Life is just a limited circle, living only with relatives – this is the edge of the cliff, standing on which is very dangerous because once you will realize that you wasted your time, tried as best as you could and haven't gained anything. The inner emptiness creates depression.

4. The limited thinking. Do you really think that your whole life consists in a couple of people? Those who live only for the family are limiting their opportunities. If you have limited your life with a couple of people this means that you have also limited your opportunities. Suppose, you have a child and a wife then you think that you only have to feed two people, care about two people, and live for two people. You see the opportunities only for two people. But, if you live for thousands of people you will look for opportunities on such a scale.

5. Ingratitude. Yes, that's true. If you only live for your family you will never teach your children to love others. That means when they leave your house they will forget about you as if you are in the past. They will have their own families, worries, and will live only for themselves. An example for children is not showing them how you live for them, but how you live for others, teaching them not to be selfish.

The value of a grain is determined by its yield, the value of a man is the benefit he can bring to others. An insect may be born, live, eat, drink, and die ... A man should live a life that will be useful to the masses.

G. Garibaldi
Italian general and politician

Do you live for Heaven or for those around you? This is up to you. I agree with the author of this statement, that everyone may be born and live for themselves, even an insect. But, the price of Eternity for a person depends on the quality of life on Earth. Do you work hard today in order to go to Heaven? It is very easy to identify that. Just answer these questions honestly:

Did I help someone today or even offer to help?

Did I hear the needs of others or was I too busy with myself?

How much time do I spend to help others? Not just talk to them but find the constructive solution to their problems?

Working hard today doesn't mean running from place to place and not allowing yourself to have some rest. Working hard is to live and to see the people around you, notice their pain, worries, becoming an answer for them but not just be another passer-by in their lives. And, believe me, when you stand before God you will not be ashamed to see the movie of your life which has not only one main character but hundreds or thousands of other people whom you helped during your life. After your death it will be so: God will show you what you have lived for and it will be bitter to see that you were standing in the queue for the discounted food, lying on the couch, or just working in the office. In the captions, you will see only a couple of people with whom you had limited your life. But infact, initially, you had a whole great life, full of years, months and days.

Summary. *Everything that you have today is your life in this very day, live it in such a way that you will not be afraid to die tomorrow.*

Vladimir Efremov is a prominent specialist in the field of artificial intelligence. He participated in the works to launch the first missiles with Yuri Gagarin into space, has contributed to the development of advanced missile systems. Four times his research team has received the State Prize.

Before his apparent death, he considered himself an absolute atheist, says Vladimir. I only trust the facts.

I had a coughing fit in my sister's house on the 12th of March. I was short of breath. My lungs didn't work properly and my heart stopped beating. From my lungs, with wheezing and foam, came out my last air. My brain flashed the thought that these are the last seconds of my life.

But, somehow I was still conscious. Suddenly there was a feeling of great lightness. There was no pain. Such a comfortable feeling I had only when I was a child. I didn't feel or see my body. I had only my feelings and memories. I was flying somewhere on a giant tube. It was a familiar feeling of flying, it had happened once before in a dream. Mentally, I tried to slow down the flight or change its direction.

There was no fear. I felt only the bliss. I tried to analyze what was happening. And, instantly a conclusion came. The

place in which I had appeared exists. If I could think then I also exist. My mind worked quite differently than before. It covered all at once and at the same time, there was neither time nor distance for it.

There is no feeling of dread, fear of death there is only the feeling that life goes on. These are the clues that help us understand that our consciousness exists and, moreover, it is more powerful than the one we had during life. Conclusions came up very quickly to mind.

I could remember the landscape without any difficulties. My memory capacity was truly amazing. I tried to go back to the place I had already flown. I visualized it. And, it worked! It seemed like teleportation. My information interaction with the surrounding gradually lost its unilateral nature. When I had a question in my mind the answer appeared immediately. At first, I accept such responses as a natural outcome of thoughts. But, the incoming information began to go beyond the knowledge I had during the life. The knowledge, I gained in this tube, was much greater than before.

Our thoughts and mind are amazing. In Heaven, everything happens at the level of thought. That is what we don't have in life here on Earth where we are unable to memorize and reproduce information in full. Tell me, which one of you is able to teleport himself today to Canada or China? It is impossible on Earth, but it is the everyday process in Heaven. And, we still confirm that there is no life outside the Earth. We hold to what is inaccessible to us,

claiming that it is the best that can be in our life. In fact, we haven't lived and seen this life. The Earth is only a partial similarity, a reduced copy of Heaven.

I realized that I was led by someone omnipresent, someone for whom there are no borders. He has unlimited possibilities, is almighty and full of love. This invisible but palpable with all my being entity did everything not to scare me. I realized that it was He who showed me all appearances and problems throughout the cause-and-effect connection. I didn't see Him but felt Him very clearly. I knew it was God...

Suddenly, I noticed that something was stopping me. I was pulled out like a carrot from its garden-bed. I didn't want to go back, everything was fine. Everything flashed and I saw my sister. She was frightened, and I was beaming with delight ... (28)

For whom do you work so hard? Who is your employer? The one thing I know is that: I live and work for Heaven and God is my employer. He gives me work on this Earth and all that I am doing today has only one concern, to work for Heaven.

We have to work hard here on Earth to have rest in Heaven after we pass on. There will be no work in Heaven. In eternity, you will be satisfied with everything that will surround you but while on Earth, we have to work hard in order to learn new information. In Heaven, our capabilities

are developed to an incredible level. We have read many stories of people, who had been there, that their mind is like the mind of the whole of humanity, and their knowledge is bigger than the one they had during their lifetime. You only need a desire in Heaven and you will learn everything. For example, a book of 500 pages: to read it you need to spend time and effort in order to understand and assimilate all that was written, but in Heaven we simply skim the information already assimilated, because the possibility of the mind is at the highest level. You do not need to go to work in Heaven. Everything can be done with the power of your thought. If you want something to eat you already have it. If you want to change your clothes this is already done. There is only fellowship, fun, new ideas, new feelings from everything that surrounds us in Heaven.

Summary. *Do not fool yourselves about your capabilities on Earth because we are limited with our desires which will disappear with the slightest difficulty in our life.*

THE HOBBY

Viktor is a mathematics teacher. He spent half of his life working in the educational system. One day a crucial moment of his life came. It was the choice of his life: should he retire or continue to work at school. No one could persuade him to stay. And, here it is retirement: when you receive money and have more time to enjoy family and hobbies. During the first week, he rested, visited his friend from another area,

went fishing with his neighbor, and then he felt complete emptiness. Viktor wilted, didn't know where to go and what to do. One day he met his children and another day he went for a walk with his wife. He felt depressed. This went on till his wife Valery had understood that her husband felt bad because he hadn't any hobbies. So she suggested to make a greenhouse and to grow vegetables to please their children and grandchildren with homemade produce. At first, they made a greenhouse in the backyard of their summerhouse, later they made beehives. In a word, their life began to spin. Viktor was respected by his neighbors and villagers. He also made a gazebo where he could spend leisure time with his friends playing dominoes and socializing in the evenings.

Before they knew it their summerhouse became their home where they had acquired a new life and hobbies.

Self-realization is a very important process for every person. That's why many of us have hobbies. Someone studies and builds a successful career, someone gets married and has children, and someone is sitting on the bench near his house and is thinking of what to do next. But, one way or another, everyone thinks about how to do their favorite thing.

On Earth, your hobby brings fun, the feeling of self-realization, importance but this is the process the pleasure of which lasts only to the moment of its fulfillment. Once the goal is achieved you set another one and try to attain it. you don't form another aim you won't be satisfied

even with the one you have reached before.

Summary. *Everyone can have fun not only from the process of achieving goals but also from everything that surrounds us in Heaven.* This is not a temporary pleasure like on Earth in Heaven our state of delight from what we see, hear, things that surround us lasts forever.

The one who finds himself, his purpose and hobby on Earth enjoys the process of self-realization. He enjoys the feeling that his wishes come true. No matter what qualities we have be it smart, beautiful, or progressive. We can realize ourselves a maximum of 5% because we won't employ the 95% of our capacity. Even the physical abilities of greatest athletes that reach incredible heights are a maximum of 15% of their capacity. We are not perfect because our mind and body are limited on Earth. Do you still have a fear of death? You can overcome it by simply visualizing eternity in Heaven in your mind.

In Heaven, our capacity will be used to 100%. Multiply your capacity on Earth by thousands of times and you will get the amount of your capacity in Heaven. It is thousands of times better than the one on Earth. Therefore, you can realize yourself for hundreds of millions of years and reach the goals you even can't imagine on Earth.

For example, you want to become a fashion designer. You try to do something, draw sketches, try to find some fabrics, learn to combine them, but you are limited by

restrictions on Earth. You have no team, no money, and no opportunity to learn from the greatest designers of the world. But in Heaven, the dream will come true and you immediately will reach the heights because you will have everything you need. You will see the colors, the existence of which you even can't imagine. You will learn new ways of sewing, ways which have never been used on Earth; you will be creating clothes embroidered with gold and diamonds. Everything will depend on your imagination.

Why are those potentials of mind and body so high in Heaven, without any efforts and restrictions? On Earth, every cell of our body is different. There are cells which live only for 1-2 days and there are others which live with a human from the very birth till death. But, the average amount of cells which die during a day is 70 billion. Therefore, there are strong and weak cells. For example, a woman becomes pregnant because the strongest sperm cell has fertilized the egg. Of the millions of sperm cells, only one reached the goal.

When we talk about the advantages of Heaven, I want to note that our body and mind will be perfect not only outside but also inside: due to the fact that all cells will be strong we also will be healthy. In Heaven, all the cells of the body will continue to exist and operate on an equal basis. There won't be inactive, weak, or dying cells, everybody will be like that one sperm. Life will not only surround our entire body, it will be also inside it.

Self-realization on Earth is only a semblance of self-realization in Heaven. During our life on Earth, everything depends on our consistency, desires, and opportunities. We often set such big goals that we don't believe in their achievement. In the process of self-realization, we also face competition with people who do not always want us to succeed or do not help to solve our problems. We also put in a lot of efforts and still we can't be sure that we will achieve our goals. There are no obstacles, misunderstandings, tears, insults, diseases, there is absolutely nothing that could stop you from achieving your goals in Heaven. In Heaven, everything works to help you achieve your desires.

Summary. *In Heaven, you can fulfill your potential and desires due to the ability of the mind and lack of personal prejudices and complexes.*

We believe that we enjoy our victories and successes on Earth, but this is only a temporary condition. The possibilities of Heaven are much more perfect than we already have. And all that is required of each of us is to overcome the fear of death and live our lives in the light of eternity.

LIVE FOR ETERNITY TODAY

"You are going to die. It may be tomorrow or fifty years from now, but sooner or later you are going to die. Even if you would rather not. Even if you have other plans. Think carefully about what you are going to do today and tomorrow and with the rest of your life."

Paulo Coelho,
Brazilian lyricist and novelist

Sooner or later we are all going to die, whether we want to or not. Therefore, we can fear death or not, it will still come. There is an easy way to overcome the fear of death. You should just understand and answer one question: What happens after I die? If you see Heaven with all its benefits then you will not be afraid to die and will enjoy life on Earth. But, if you see the darkness and eternity in Hell then hurry to change your lifestyle and serve the Lord with all your heart, soul, and mind. Do we think about what we can do for our eternity today? Tomorrow may never come, but we have today to do something in order to reach Heaven. Are we looking for the opportunities to overcome the fear of death and acquire the interest in eternity?

To free ourselves from fear of death is:
- To think about Heaven every day.
- Live on Earth only in order to spread the word of Heaven among people and live for Heaven.

Each of us has TODAY, and everyone uses it differently. Someone thinks of old times and feels sorry about things he couldn't achieve. Someone lives in the future, dreams, and makes plans for tomorrow. It turns out that none of us live today, it remains outside our plans. There is only past which can't be turned back, there may be future that has not yet become. But, it is TODAY that many of us do not have. Today is the way it is, that's all. We put off our dreams, desires, and aspirations for some abstract future that may never come. We think: "Tomorrow will be a better time." but this "tomorrow" may never come. It is "today" that we have to do those things we want to do. We always think tomorrow will be fine and everything will change for the better. But, you know it very well that is just not true.

Summary. *Living life for Heaven today is to focus your actions on meeting the needs of others.*

Hobbies, that we talked about earlier, will be your favorite if it is in demand of others. For example, let's say your hobby is to play with children. It is good. You will enjoy the process and get the pleasure of being close to children. Within a year, two, or five, your children will have other needs. What will happen with your hobby? If you want, you can implement it in a kindergarten, work with children, or be a volunteer in an orphanage. Then you will see that you have lived many of your "today" for your children and after deciding to live for a number of children who are in need of your love you decide to live for Heaven. And, who knows, maybe many of them will become full of life, goal-oriented

personalities; thanks to your love. That is what it means to live for Heaven but not only for yourself. It means to share beautiful things you already have, to make someone happy, to see those who need your kindness today.

Let's not live «tomorrow» but take the responsibility today in order to become a part of Heaven. It is worth trying:

Be attentive to details. We hurry up our living, run to the meetings, are late for work and do not notice anyone or anything that is around us. Besides that, we do not see how beautiful this day is and how many special little things are going on during this day. We need to learn from children which see even in an ordinary day so many unusual things which make them happy. And everyone around is infected with this happiness. Want to be happy start to focus and see the details.

Enjoy the little things. We want all at once- a big salary, an absolute love of family and friends, good health. But perfection does not exist. That's why you should be grateful even for little surprises and pleasant things. Even the smile of a passerby should please you today.

Share your happiness with others. To be happy is your decision. You have the right to be happy and give this happiness to everyone around you. Do not be a consumer waiting until someone makes you happy.

We have TODAY and should make someone happy today, living daily for Heaven. In eternity, happiness is a state of heart, sight, and communication. In a word, everything that surrounds us brings happiness once we touch it. On Earth, you can be happy at home but even the weather can change your mood. We live on Earth and think that this is all our happiness, but no, it is only a small opportunity to understand what happiness can really be.

If we realize what Heaven is and what benefits it conceals, we must follow it. The legacy of Heaven is to become a person who is willing to live every moment of his life on Earth in order to reach Heaven and its reality. We will discuss this in the final chapter of the book and now let's recall main points we have learned:

1. The work on Earth is fun for few of us. It is perceived as a necessity of life. But, in Heaven there is no such concept as "work", you only do what you like or enjoy. There is no such thing as "an impossible mental labor". Everything you want to know will be given to you easily.

2. Your hobbies on Earth require some efforts. It often falls apart if you have no money, opportunities, or time. But in Heaven, hobbies are a perfection which you can unleash and live the way you like without any limitations of the mind, body, or time.

3. We all have today and we can live it either for ourselves or for Heaven. Living for Heaven is to live for those who are around you. That means for the people we do not normally notice, living in the illusion of our employment. But, if we decide today to live for eternity, then this process can be stopped only by the absence of our actions. Sharing happiness is to distribute it with every breath of our bodies.

GOLDEN TRUTH

• You can just live your life the way you want, and at the end of your years discover the evidence that Heaven exists, but then it will be impossible to change anything, there is no turning back, and you can't be wise after death.

• Live your life the way that your affairs, actions and words even after the sudden tragic end of life on Earth, can acquire a life in Heaven.

• Everyone may be born and live for themselves, even an insect but the price of Eternity for a person depends on the quality of life on Earth.

• Working hard is to live and to see the people around you, notice their pain, worries, and become an answer for them. But not just being another passerby in their lives.

• There are no obstacles, misunderstandings, tears, insults, diseases, absolutely nothing that could stop you from achieving goals in Heaven– on the contrary, everything contributes to the achievement of your desires.

• Everyone can have fun not only from the process of achieving goals but also from everything that surrounds us in Heaven.

Test
"What matters in my life?"

In each statement or question of the test, there should be only one answer. Next to each answer, in brackets, is a score. Your result of the test corresponds to the obtained amount of points.

1. Does your job bring you pleasure?
a) No. (1)
b) There is no pleasure in it, I work like a horse. (0)
c) It depends on how I work. (2)
d) Yes. (3)

2. What or who brings you joy?
   a) Profit (1)
   b) Favorite food (0)
   c) The family (2)
   d) All around me makes me happy (3)

3. When you rush home after a hard day, do you notice the people around you?
   a) No, I even don't see the ground under my feet (1)
   b) I see the faces of people (0)
   c) I try all my best to notice everything (2)
   d) Yes. I am attentive to those around me (3)

4. Your life is based on ...
    a) The financial benefit (1)
    b) The compliance of desires (0)
    c) The welfare of your family (2)
    d) The possibility of being useful to people
       around you (3)

5. Who makes you a happy person?
    a) I don't know. The one who helped me
       with something (1)
    b) Nobody (0)
    c) My family (2)
    d) Myself (3)

RESULTS
OF THE TEST

Less than 5 points. Your life is based on a position of the consumer. You do not see people around you or yourself in these people. Unfortunately, with the direction your life is going, you will never reach or even see Heaven. Do not delay; start seeing yourself as a human being, a lot depends on you, and future of your life and family is very paramount.

6-10 points. You don't relieve yourself from the responsibility for your life but also don't assume that you can affect someone's choice. Living for Heaven - is to spread your attention not only on yourself but also on those who are nearby. Today, you already had the knowledge that can be shared with those who have not gained it yet. Let Heaven be your way of thinking, a way of life through the love showed to others.

11-15 points. Your life is not limited to personal or family needs. You understand that in order to become a part of Heaven – you should now become the answer for those who are close to you, and it's not only the family but all those people with whom you communicate with. Keep reading the book, form your knowledge of Heaven to become a part of you and let it continue to guide the way you live.

PRACTICAL
TASKS

1. Does your work really bring you pleasure?

2. What would you do if you had a lot of money?

3. What sphere of influence would you choose? What are the problems of your country or city that you would love to solve?

"The Illusion of employment." –is the recommended book by the University of Life. Do not spend days, months and years on illusion, because life will not change, and the time will pass unnoticed. Appreciate your life now and at long last you will gain Heaven.

Chapter 9

ACCEPT THE TRUE
LEGACY OF HEAVEN

Chapter 9
ACCEPT THE TRUE LEGACY OF HEAVEN

Dear reader, throughout this book we have brought up many important issues like death's advantage, the existence of life after death, also that our life on Earth is just a great preparation for life in Heaven. In the previous chapter, we have figured out that our life on Earth no matter how beautiful is incomplete because of Earthly limitations, but in Heaven a pleasant surprise is waiting for us as we are not limited and can become who we want. But, to get to Heaven, we must work hard here on Earth, affecting the people we encounter daily positively.

Summary. *Heaven is available for everyone who wants to attain it, and everyone that is able to comprehend it.*

God gives an equal right for every person to become part of life in Heaven, but we cannot exercise it without defeating the FEAR OF DEATH, not even starting to live here on Earth. We ourselves choose the way and there are two options.

First. Accept God in your heart, saying a prayer of repentance from sins, and start living for Him, helping others. In this case, we automatically become heirs of Heaven, this is our goal.

Second. You live for yourself, thinking that you have not done anything wrong, just living like everyone else. You hold on to life as your last chance not seeing the continuation of your life in death. At the same time, deep down inside, you believe that God exists, but you are not ready to change today, to live for someone else. In this case, you are living in illusion and wasting time on your assumptions about Heaven and eternity, thinking that there is plenty of time.

HEAVEN – EARTH'S MORE POTENT REALITY

Life is a dangerous thing. It leads to death.

Stanisław Jerzy Lec,
outstanding Polish satirist

Do you still believe that you are living, or have the confidence that the real life will begin in Heaven? Both life and death are inevitable for us, and knowing this, I'm certainly going to think today about what will happen after my life on Earth. Let your eternity derail because of your disbelief or doubt it at the very least. Putting the life we have now in opposite to the one we will attain after death, we make a choice with obvious consequences. But, still, I suggest the further discovery of the beauty of eternity. After all, Heaven is the only reality of a full life

ETERNITY IS THE ONLY THING WORTH LIVING FOR, IT IS THE ONLY TRUTH, ALL THE REST IS FALSE. Life is an endless process of survival and competition during which the person does not stop, in order to live. It can seem that a rich person, say Steve Jobs, could live happily, but work took up all his time and there was no time for living before the news about a deadly disease did not show him that not everything is in mans' control and that money is good, but Eternity is more valuable.

If work, then only for the sake of Heaven. If earn, then only for the sake of Heaven, and not for your own pleasures. For example, even if you do not see the sense in making a million then I can tell you that it is not necessary for you, but for you to serve other people with this money. Well, how can you feed the needy, if you are living from paycheck to paycheck, how can you dress the poor, if you are dressing on second-hand clothes? Everything you do during your life on Earth for other people will be returned to you in a repeatedly multiplied equivalent in Heaven. For example, someone from his labor on Earth builds castles and estates, and others will get a one-room apartment. Relevance does not depend on how much land you have plowed, but on how many people you led to salvation and reconciliation with God. So, even receiving your one-room apartment, you will not envy the one who will receive the palace as an award. After all, life in Heaven is based on love, and not on mercantile requirements.

Life on Heaven is very different from the Earthly one. We have already ascertained that all our thoughts about eternity is nothing at all; we should rather think and see Heaven as the only benefit of our lives. The beauty of Heaven is there for a good reason, God has prepared the best for his faithful children for those who did not waste their life on Earth, but worked hard to receive a reward in Heaven. This contrast is necessary for us to appreciate and wish to attain the beauty of Heaven, to live and enjoy all the opportunities that we did not know about during our Earthly journey.

The contrast of life in Heaven and Earth can be compared, for example, to a limited and poor choice of clothing during the Soviet era everybody wore gray or blue suits, brown dresses. Notwithstanding the situation, there was an abundance of clothes of various colors abroad. Those Soviet people who had the opportunity to go to other countries abroad, were shocked with the choice of goods available on the shelves of foreign shops. Or, for example, imagine that you know only about the existence of television in black and white and suddenly you get to see the video in 4D wouldn't you be speechless with surprise and delight? These examples are a good illustration of the fact that the contrast is really striking: how insignificant is our life on Earth, but how beautiful is the real life in Heaven. We hold on to all Earthly things, without even knowing how insignificant and petty they are compared to what you can have in eternity in Heaven.

Still thinking and what about communication with loved ones on Earth and the life without them in Heaven? But, here I am ready to show you that the only reality of life is the true life in eternity. On Earth, we are limited in communication, having it only with those who are available to us or those who are pleasant and do not bring us resentment and disappointment and do not hurt our pride. But in Heaven, there is only one available feeling; love that generates joy, happiness, tenderness, warmth, concern, respect. So there we will communicate with everyone and it does not matter what the status of these people are.

I almost forgot. Do you chat with the animals on Earth? Well, yes, you talk to them, but they do not answer you. In Heaven, not only animals will talk to you, but even trees and flowers. All that surrounds you: every flower, bush, or grass will not just talk but keep the conversation interesting, joke, and have fun. Imagine a picture- you drive on a ski with bears or swim in the warm sea with the whales. Animals will not be wild; they will understand you as you will them.

The reality of Heaven is not in the events that will determine where you want to be or what you want to feel, but you decide upon it. For example, if you want to find yourself in the winter, summer or fall, you can through thoughts go to the place of a certain season of the year and feel it. In addition, with your thoughts, you will be able to enter wherever you want, and see with your own eyes all that is happening all over the Earth. We have not once

mentioned the super abilities of Heaven; they are as real, as real as your life today.

That in Heaven we will be able to communicate with people and everything that surrounds us and we will feel their joy and happiness as our own. Isn't it wonderful to have such a life in which there is no place for boredom? Spending time to live and enjoy life. Only Heaven is worth living.

What a pity the only way to Heaven is in a hearse.

Stanisław Jerzy Lec,
outstanding Polish satirist

Funny thing, right? Nevertheless, the way for each of us will be determined by the life we lived on Earth. Someone's body will be carried in the hearse, but the soul will inherit Heaven, and someone on the same hearse will proceed to Hell. Therefore, I see the daily reality of Heaven to which I aspire with my every deed and every action today.

Summary. *Do not plan to live «someday" life is already happening today in every decision you make.*

THERE IS NO LIFE ON EARTH

Into the world I came, but Heaven was not disturbed.
I died, but the radiance of lights was not multiplied.
And, nobody told me why was I born
And, why my life was hastily torn.
Omar Khayyam, Persian writer, philosopher

We are born without our planning, we live up to twenty years trying to plan our life, we pair off and get married. But is this all to life? Home, work, vanity, children, streets, friends ... In short, life is not ours, but we are fiercely trying to prove that the owners of our own destiny are us. Nonetheless, during the whole of our lives, we blame someone else for the difficulties, for the lack of opportunities, for the lack of help and prompting. We reject the existence of God, and even if we believe, we do not rely on Him entirely; we doubt and then have to live anyhow. Can this vicious circle of vanity be called life? I am going to give examples for finer illustration, draw yourself a picture of your «life» right now if you think this is life:

What is the point of your life today? In whom will this life continue? Will there be an echo of your life fifty years after your death? Who will remember you in hundred years?

We pretend that we live. But agreeing that this is life does not mean seeing a full life. For example, you think that the point of life is money. You learn in school, dreaming

about a rich life, you make efforts, discover new things, set goals for your education and enter the university, which will give you a boost for takeoff. You reach the top of career and finally get the long-awaited financial freedom. But, will this make you happy? Will you gain life in its entirety? Will you attain Heaven? After all, life is acquired when it is multiplied, when you give it to another person, when you are not throwing this life around left and right, appealing only to yourself, but when you multiply it in others. Great multipliers of their life are Mother Teresa, Martin Luther King Jr, Nick Vujicic; these are the great benefactors of the world, such as Bill and Melinda Gates, George Soros, and many others. They become the ones who attain life not due to their wealth and their business. THERE IS NO LIFE IN BECOMING WEALTHY, LIFE IS WHEN WE ADD VALUE TO SOMEONE'S LIFE.

For example, you think that the point of life is to pair off or get married. Well, you have matured for this decision and you have even found the person who is willing to share life with you. But, does your life lie in another person, will he or she be responsible for your life, will he or she fill your expectations? Tell me, is this life to get another person for which you have to decide everything? Is this life to run around and think, «How will my wife perceive my coming late from work» or «what will my husband think if I don't make dinner?» This is not life, it is an additional burden for those who hurry to get married or try to hide in it. You need to listen, you to need to pay attention, you need to feed, and in this case what about enjoying life? Will you enjoy life? Practice shows that a relationship was just an illusion if it quickly breaks down by the reality of marriage. If it were otherwise there would be no terrible statistics of divorces in families. It is simple: there is no life in relying on another person even if they are close. There you are and God Who gave you life, so for solving the problems and difficulties ask yourself and God and do not load your husband or wife with all your inner turmoil, demanding an answer from them.

Summary. *Life is not about getting married. This is an opportunity to give and not to take, an opportunity to love in spite of everything, and not to expect that your partner will change for you.*

There is no life if you are not ready to devote yourself without expecting anything in return.

For example, you assume that life is to give birth to a child. Let's say you become pregnant. Do you think that bringing in a child will give you happiness? You have given birth and at this time you stop your life for a couple of years to live entirely for a little human being. Then work to support, to provide, and not to deprive this little person of anything. But, it may not take some time and the child may eventually tell you, «You haven't given me anything at all» and leave your life. You will remain with your unfulfilled plans, with the lost years of life, but you have already given part of your life to the child, only one child.

Summary. *There is no life in children there is guidance and the ability to pass all that you have discovered and what you have acquired to your children.*

Life is not in a child's birth; life is in the millions of people around you who will carry the flame of your life forever. One child is good, but after twenty years after your death no one will remember you, but the millions of people to whom you have passed a piece of your life to and after two hundred years people will know who you have been and what you have done for humanity.

There is no life on Earth, all these are only the fragments that give us a reference point on what can be a real life in Heaven.

What they do in Heaven we are ignorant of what they do not we are told expressly: that they neither marry nor are given in marriage.

Jonathan Swift,
Anglo-Irish satirist

Do not think that life in Heaven is an everyday process: it is exciting and full of incredible histories of LIFE for eternity.

Life is a form of matter. Existence is characterized by high structural complexity, the ability to process the resources of the environment, evolve, resist the decay, and replicate.

Are you replicating, if you believe that you are living? In Heaven, the process of self-reproduction exists in everything starting from the generation of ideas and ending with their full implementation.

Life on Earth is just an example of the life that will be perfect in Heaven.

Summary. *The true success is only in Heaven, prosperity in everything you want to come across, success in every idea and its implementation.*

Life is in Heaven, the Earth is just a vapor, so you should not hold on to what will be gone. OVERCOME THE FEAR OF DEATH with new opportunities of true life in Eternity!

DON'T LET IGNORANCE ROB YOU OF YOUR LEGACY

The Parable « Get Up! »

One student asked his Sufi teacher:

Teacher, what would you say if you discovered about my fall?

— Get up!

— And, the next time?

— Again get up!

— And, for how long will all the falls and get ups continue?

— Fall and get up, as long as you are alive! For someone who has fallen and not risen is dead.

This parable shows us that we have to stand up and look only towards Heaven, towards a life which is not limited only to our Earthly existence. Today is another day to humble yourself and say to yourself: «I do not know what's next. This is a good step, a prompting to rise up and do it the right way now. Get up every time you fall and every time unbelief comes to you. Get up every time you sin, get up every time you are in doubt, get up every

time it is hard for you to walk and relax in the way of life, get up no matter what. The only thing you have to do is to get up and continue your journey to a full life in Heaven.

Life in Heaven is our legacy from God, it is the gift that every man was left with after the death of Jesus Christ. The only thing we need is to become His son or daughter to inherit it. But often, we are looking for an Earthly legacy, which is temporary in life.

Now, nobody will be surprised with the dismissive attitude of children towards their parents. Let's assume the parents are still alive and have an apartment, and the children are already dividing among themselves who will inherit the living space. Why is this happening? It is simple: they know that they are children and therefore, heirs of all that their parents have achieved over the years of their life. But why then do so few people tend to take on the legacy of the One who gave the life itself? After all, parents are those who gave birth, who carried a fetus, who fathered the child, but God is the one who gives life. Then why demand from parents our inheritance; the apartments, villas, or land we do not demand from the Creator of life and His legacy?

Summary. *Because of our ignorance, we lose the true legacy that is measured not by the cost of apartments, cars, or small bank account.*

In Heaven, all this will be equated to a single penny anyway. As we said, even Heaven's roads are lined with

gold, emeralds, and jewelry. Indeed, life can be in such abundance compared to the part of the parents' flat on Earth? We neglect the true legacy, why do you not seek to attain it and why do you not think about eternity?

We are used to living for Earthly cares: study, go to work, get married, have a baby, and again work, caring for grandchildren, aging and the end finally comes. But, do we ever stop somewhere between our birth and death to think about eternity? We only consider it if suddenly a time of grief or disaster arises, at this time, we stop thinking about ourselves, but about God, and we start looking for help.

If God has not «floored us» from time to time, we would have no time to look at the sky.

Blaise Pascal,
French mathematician, physicist

This is true: God allows the difficulties and suffering for us to stop and think about eternity, about accepting his legacy. So, if you're down on your shoulders today, thank God for the opportunity and privilege to accept the legacy of the Father, and not to live in anticipation of the human heritage. If you decide to accept this legacy, then you must understand that you have taken responsibility for it. After all, the truth is: if the children abandon their parents and do not help them, do not hurry to come and help, do not care about them, often these parents find someone who will be of help to them, and as a reward, these people will

receive the inheritance that «should» have belonged to their children. The same is with God: if He allows life's difficulties to come to you, get up to honor Him as a Father, get up, to live for Him, take care of His heart's desire through the reading of His Word, the Bible. Become a son or daughter of God. The word «become» expresses an action, and means doing something, rather than hoping for a miracle. «Become» is the position, rather than waiting, and the one who will become the son or daughter of God, will receive the legacy from our Heavenly Father. Legacy is a passing of all that the parents achieved, it is an act of presenting their children with everything starting with knowledge and ending with material possessions. The legacy of Heaven will be accepted by the one who did not live a life of vanity or a life of concerns, but lived clearly, deliberately, knowing about the legacy, doing the deeds for the people and for your Heavenly Father.

The way we live, does it look like the life of people who will accept the legacy? Does it happen that we want to act but the slightest difficulty or reluctance to go contrary to our expectation blows us from the path of the legacy? Devotion to your task regardless of the external stimuli here's an example of a man who knows what he is doing and knows where he is going.

At a time, when America was still a British colony, in that area, which later became known as the State of Connecticut, the colonial legislature was sitting. Suddenly the sunlight faded and everything was shrouded in darkness.

Someone shouted, «This is the end of the world! Everybody go home, and get ready!»

But, one of the member of the Legislative Assembly, the old deacon, stood up and said: «Brothers, maybe this is the Judgment's Day, I do not know. The Lord indeed may come. But, when He comes, I want Him to catch me in my place; I want to perform my duty till the last minute. Mr. Chairman, I make a proposal to bring the candles and to continue handling the colony affairs» (29)

A man who lives for a legacy, will not go astray, he will not lose his estate because of the difficulties or anxiety that came upon him. Never let the ignorance of your legacy take control over your life and deprive you of the highest award, a reward of Heaven. As much as we would like, but it is impossible to compare the Eternal life in perfection with the Earth award, which is measured only in some conventional units. The richness and benefit of Heaven are incomparable to our possible gains on the Earth.

THE GREAT REWARD OF HEAVEN

The man, who has done a worthy deed, will never receive less than he gave.

Henry Ward Beecher,
American religious leader

What does the reward mean? The reward is a special gratitude, a badge of honor that marks the person's merits. So, not even one of your worthy deeds will be ignored, there will be no such case that you have done good, and it came around to you with evil. But, you may rise in revolt, that is the way things usually happens in relationships with people, do good and you get back evil. Yes, it happens in relationships with people, but not with God. We may not receive the right response after we have done good for a person, but we may get it from another, the one you do not owe anything at all. This is a kind of the law of sowing and reaping: what you do in your life, will be returned to you.

Summary. *A reward awaits you. You reap what you have sown in this world and nobody who has done good will not be rewarded.*

You will be judged in Heaven by all your actions on Earth. God is fair, and there will not be such situations that you worked, plowed, helped people, society, the world with your last strength, and coming to Heaven, will get only a modest estate, exactly the same the one who could only help his relatives and loved ones. No, the reward system in Heaven is in multiple levels, as well as on the Earth: one gets rewards, some titles, and some medals and plaques. In Heaven, also there is a grading of legacy.

It is expressed this way. Let's say you spend your money on good deeds, fed the needy, helped to raise funds for people's operations, were attentive to those who lived

nearby, to those who were suffering you were the answer to their lives. In Heaven, you will get your reward, for example, the palace with properties, forests, gardens, animals, and birds. And, those who lived for their family, went to church, respected their parents, in short, lived and did not sin. So, getting to Heaven, he too will receive his reward, a one-room apartment. In addition, skills and opportunities, and more precisely their level, will also be different, for example, someone wants to bring ideas and innovation, and he does it, and someone will not be given such an opportunity because the level of the ability he has earned is lower. But, do you know the best of it? In Heaven, there will be no envy, or resentment, or greed because everything there will be steeped with love. Both the first and second person from the above-mentioned example will be satisfied with what they have, and will be able to fully enjoy life in Heaven.

Marvin Ford was in the hospital after a serious heart attack. He has experienced clinical death.

I saw such a dazzling spectacle that I had never seen and could not even imagine in my entire life! The beauty, the greatness, the splendor of the city was breathtaking! The golden color and the rays of light that came from everywhere were blinding, but not my eyes.

The beauty that you have never seen in your life ... Nothing can compare with what you will see in Heaven, no spectacle or the appearance of the world can be compared with the beauty of Heaven. In the testimonies

of eyewitnesses, there are tips that the cities that exist on Earth, are also there in Heaven. Earth is the image of Heaven, it looks similar to Heaven. Today you can see the cities, the countries, different continents, and you know they also are there in Heaven.

I have seen the walls of jasper! They were absolutely clear because the light from the inside of the city was so bright that absolutely nothing could stand against him. And, I saw in the walls' foundation the precious and semi-precious stones. Pearly gates looked as if they had at least 1,500 kilometers in diameter. And, I saw from wall to wall, streets covering millions of kilometers of solid gold. They were not paved with gold, as the poet wrote; no Heavenly Streets consisted of solid gold, completely and totally transparent.

Gold on Earth is just a piece of jewelry that people are so fond of. All the streets in Heaven are paved with gold, imagine: you go and see how the street beckons you with its beauty and grandeur. There are jewels in the walls, not the bricks or stones, but real emeralds, rubies, and pearls. Well, how can this superiority be compared to what we have seen or known on Earth? We think we have seen something or known something, in fact, it is nothing at all.

Oh, what a splendor and beauty, and the rays of light that came from these streets! And, I saw on each side of the street mansion made of gold. I saw huge manors and small houses; I saw the houses of all sizes in between. As a builder, I'm interested in architecture and materials, and I am

good in buildings. I examined all the details in this city even more than the city itself, to learn what these houses were built. And, do you know what? I could not find any settings! All of them were complete. They've all been ready! (30)

Mansions, houses, manors of gold. Are you still afraid of losing your one or two-room bedroom in the suburb of the city? In Heaven where everything is ready for us in perfection, you can live a lot better life than you are living now. These houses were in store for us, we do not need to take a loan, or wait, that someone will help us or leave a legacy to live in your house. In Heaven, everything exists to bring you pleasure.

Jesus said, «*In my Father's house are many rooms. And, if it were not so, I would have told you that I go to prepare a place for you. If I go and prepare a place for you, I will come again and receive you to Myself, that where I am there you may be also.*» (*In the 14th chapter of John*).

Jesus did his duty. He expects that we will do ours. He expects us to fulfill our end of the bargain.

Summary. *All that we can get or have on Earth depends on the effort, resources, and inner pain experienced. But in Heaven, we can have everything we want, as a legacy from God the Father.*

On Earth, every moment of our life we are responsible: for ourselves, for our family, for our children, and in some cases for our parents. In order to have something, one needs to constantly maintain a high level of responsibility. In Heaven, there is no such thing as responsibility. Are you not surprised? After all, the quality of our life on Earth depends on how we exercise our responsibility: the one who is responsible for himself and his future, lives and does not merely exist. For example; while living, we go to school. The way we treat this process of education will determine a few things. There are those who were simply «rubbing their pants,» and there are those who were «grinding away at their studies». The responsibility for your education today will affect the future. Yes, maybe the one who did not study has the wealth and money, he may even buy a degree, but will he be a man of quality is the question. But the one who has studied and acquired knowledge, has been responsible for everything that came in his life, will become a professional, the man of results and success. So, returning to the subject of Heaven, we need to understand that plowing and staying in constant pursuit of success as we are here on Earth but living and enjoying we will in Heaven. The way we live and how we serve on Earth, that will we get hitting the court of God. In Heaven, the grace of God is in abundance.

Grace is an abundance of Earthly blessings, blessed place. This definition gives us a vocabulary, but tell me, isn't it great? We practically are not able to reach it living on Earth. You may ask what a paradox? Look, you have earned a thousand, your needs will immediately grow

up to two thousand, you earn a million, you will want to have a house costing two million. You strived for a successful marriage, and there you have it, the love of your life, but ... Already after one year of your family life something will not be good enough for you. You dreamed of a prestigious job, and you got it, but something still is not the way you imagine it. That is how the world is arranged. Not all people are able to get pleasure from the minimum benefits. Inflated expectations do not bring us the pleasure of life on Earth that is why it is not a fertile place for a full life. Heaven is that place, and there are no:

evaluation of your consistency

envy for other people

inner concerns that something might be wrong

condemnation of your actions and the actions of others

futility, as any business or idea brings productive results

Heaven is a beneficial place where there is an abundance of wholesome, interesting and exciting life. And the way we live our lives on Earth, can bring success and enjoyment in Eternity. If you still harbor the fear of death. OVERCOME THIS FEAR with your belief in eternal life.

The difference between life on Earth and in Heaven can be compared to the hard work of a man in the field. On a hot, sultry day, he plows the ground hard and tirelessly until the sun burns his body. He knows that this day would come and go and a cool evening will follow, and with it the long-awaited rest, during which he will regain his strength. So, this is hard work and there is life on Earth, and this evening, rest, and enjoyment is life in Heaven.

We are really working hard to survive, but we do this differently there are those who work on themselves, cultivating their personality, helping others, and there are those who just plow and do not enjoy the fruits of their labor. But what we get, thanks to our work on Earth is just money that quickly diminishes, giving it to someone who earns on us. But in Heaven we get the joy of communication, fulfillment of any desires, the realization of cherished dreams, communication with people, whom we previously did not know, and could hear of their greatness and ministry.

ALL YOU NEED — IS TO INHERIT HEAVEN

The essence of every faith is in that it gives such meaning to life, which can be destroyed only by death

Leo Tolstoy,
Russian writer, and thinker

In Hamlet's Soliloquy, there was one question that we are asking up to now, trying to show his indecision: «To be or not to be ....» With this episode, I would like to ask you, dear reader, «To live or not to live? That is the question». This issue is still relevant today, and after your death. For the answer, you must determine today to assess the results of your choice after death. As the great master of literature, Leo Tolstoy said, life has meaning and continuation only when this life features faith. Do you believe, dear friends that you are living, or somewhere amid the hectic days you come to realize that there was no life and the fear of death overcomes you more and more with each day? If you want to live and to realize what you are living for, what are you seeking, you will need to acquire the faith, faith in eternity, faith in God, faith in Jesus Christ, Who died for us, that we could live in Heaven.

Summary. *The fear of death can be overcome when you do not believe in death, but in life itself after death.*

Faith is our way to the legacy of Heaven, it is our guideline on Earth, our beacon of life. Faith is what was given to us through the great cost of the life of Jesus Christ; the Son of God, and this has made us absolutely free. What does it mean to live and be free from the fear of death? It means wearing yourself every day on Earth. Wearing yourself is not carrying unsaid words of love. It is thanksgiving to those we meet on our life's path, words of admiration for those who are successful at least in something, words of forgiveness to those who cannot tell

them themselves. Wearing yourself is not about concealing resentment, but forgiving people, wearing yourself is not about accumulating knowledge, money, opportunities, but giving it to all those who need it. Wearing yourself is to acknowledge the people who are close to you in the same apartment, in a stairwell, in one city, in one country.

TO INHERIT HEAVEN IS TO SOW YOURSELF FOR OTHER PEOPLE, NOT TO PURSUE THE EARTHLY BENEFITS, WHICH ARE ANYWAY CORRUPTIBLE. This does not mean that you need to live like a tramp, because the tramp Johnny and deputy Johnny are two different people with very different levels of influence and tell me who will be able to change at least their city; a tramp Johnny or a deputy Johnny? I don't urge you to live in poverty or, after receiving a salary, to give it all to someone who needs it. No, I'm saying we should live not for ourselves, but for Heaven.

Not knowing the truth about Heaven, not knowing how beautiful life in Heaven is, man thinks that he lives when he is just walking on Earth, and he thinks that this is the best thing in his life. Walking the usual path to the shop near his house, he drives through the same route to work, meets his relatives at home and again the next day is the same as the previous one. But, this is not life.

Summary. *True life begins in Heaven, where every moment is like a new discovery, a new victory, or a great success, and we live on Earth, to inherit the eternity of God the Father.*

It is written in the Bible, «Set your affection on things above, not on things on the Earth.» Pursuing vanity, life's problems and a whole lot of things distracts us from life after physical death. Do not allow yourself or anyone else to steal your life in Heaven. Your life may be stolen in case you do not know anything about the eternity when you do not cherish the thought of Heaven when you do not care WHAT WILL HAPPEN AFTER YOUR DEATH.

After inheriting Heaven, work will no longer be needed, we will share our successes. We will discuss the challenges encountered on Earth on our life's path to Heaven. We will be pleased by the Earthly successes and victories we scored each time we made decisions towards gaining eternity in Heaven. The Angels in Heaven, will show us pictures of the periods they ministered to us, the circumstances they helped us through, and how they secured us for a full life in Heaven. We will watch movies about the way things happened in our life, our doubts and our strength. Our victories and the victories of the great servants of God in Heaven will be available to see in its fullness.

While living on Earth, and all we do is just striving for material things, these might bring meaning to our life, but the essence of Eternity is that in Heaven all these

achievements will be used in other to enjoy life. For example, after the end of the day, we hurry to get home faster, especially when it's cold outside, and rain or snow envelops our body, we dream about how to get home and warm up in the kitchen with a cup of hot tea. But, coming home, we no longer dream about it, because it is true. The same with Heaven: it is already there, and the only thing that is required of us is to dream and with all our life and actions to achieve its perfection. Everyone is now on the way, but home in Heaven will only be reached by the people who understand what they have lived for. Heaven will be reached only by those who knew that after death they will inherit Heaven in all its beauty and splendor.

What will happen after our death is the real and genuine life. We must decide if we want to gain eternal life or only live for Earthly pleasures... I think that this issue is no longer a dilemma for you. We will have to conform our choice every day and every moment to the standards of Heaven if our choice is to gain eternity in Heaven.

GOLDEN TRUTHS

• To reach Heaven, we must live for eternity, work hard for Heaven here on Earth, for the good of people

• Heaven is available to everybody who wants to attain it, there is no one who cannot comprehend it

• Heaven is the only thing worth living for, the only thing that is real, everything else is a mirage

• The reality of Heaven lies in the fact that not the events will determine where you want to be or what you want to feel, but you

• In Heaven, we will be able to truly, fully communicate with people, experiencing their joy, their happiness as our own

• Do not plan to start living «sometimes later» the decision is in your hands. Decide to start living today

• Life is lived meaningfully with a possible continuance after death only if there is a belief in Eternal life

• To inherit Heaven is to scatter yourself for other people, and not to chase the benefit of the world that are perishable

• Do not allow yourself or someone else to steal your life in Heaven

TEST
«MY LEGACY»

In each statement or question of the test, there should be only one answer. Next to each answer, in brackets, is a score. Your result of the test corresponds to the obtained amount of points.

1. **What does the reality of Heaven mean to you ?**
   a) Only things that I can see (1)
   b) The clouds (0)
   c) My desire for eternal life (2)
   d) A full life in eternity (3)

2. **When the need arises to share your knowledge with those who do not yet know, what will be your reaction?**
   a) I will never do this (1)
   b) I will be offended (0)
   c) Of course, I love to teach (2)
   g) I will see that I play an important role in someone's life (3)

3. If you are asked for advice as a successful person, would you share your secrets for free?
  a) No (1)
  b) Never, everything has its price (0)
  c) I'll tell, but not all of them (2)
  d) I will share everything I know (3)

4. What do you need to do today to live in Heaven?
  a) Hurry up living (1)
  b) Never sin (0)
  c) To live for those who are near (2)
  d) Serve other people with all that I have (3)

5. Are you ready to pay the price on Earth, to attain the legacy of Heaven?
  a) It depends on the price of the issue (1)
  b) A bird in the hand is worth two in the bush (0)
  c) I think I could (2)
  d) I'm already paying the price for Eternity (3)

RESULTS
OF THE TEST

Less than 5 points. Unfortunately, your concept of Eternity is based only on what you see or what surrounds you. Having no idea of what Heaven is, it will be hard for you to live. So, attain this belief within yourself. Examine your life and begin to live by faith in what you will receive today.

6-10 points. You are on the way to your legacy of Heaven. You know exactly what to do and how to live today, to attain Heaven, but you should not just get this knowledge, but also practice them in your normal life. Studying the possibilities of Heaven, do not limit them in your imagination, share this knowledge with everyone around you.

11-15 points. You are an heir of Heaven. Your lifestyle is not determined by your desires, and you are guided in your decisions by Heaven's values. You are ready to pay the price for your attainments for others also become as you are. To enrich yourself even more, so that you always have something to give to people who are close to you.

PRACTICAL
TASKS

1. What is the legacy you wish to leave to your loved ones?

2. What prevents you from becoming an heir of Heaven today? What resources do you lack to fully live today for Heaven? How can they be attained?

3. What is the meaning of your life? Who enjoys your presence? Who enriches his life due to you? Write a list of these people, pointing out whom they take you for and the special things you do for them.

Recommended book of UNIVERSITY OF LIFE «10 questions to Vladimir Pozner and all thinking people.» Acknowledging your limitations in the choices of your life on Earth, we are opening the gates of Heaven into our lives, and understanding the value of the One, Who has defined our life is God.

CLOSING REMARKS

Dear reader, here we come to the end of our amazing journey to heaven. Will you succeed in overcoming your fear of death due to the information received about the beauty of eternity in Heaven. Surely, you may not understand everything, but I will say one thing: one who doesn't see his/her future only lives an ordinary life. There is no point in wasting your time and resources on fear, especially the fear that is inevitable for each of us. We all will die, but will we receive eternal life when we die? This is a question for all of us to answer and the decision is ours.

"The bad news is time flies. The good news is you're the pilot."

Michael Altshuler
Motivational Speaker and Professional Sales Trainer

Time flies ahead of us if we are not the pilot of our life, if we give the steering wheel of our life to circumstances, the opinion of others, the words and the difficulties that knock at our door every day. The one who manages his life, who holds the steering wheel of his time, lives his life to the fullest. The kind of life you will live on Earth, depends only on you. And even the question, whether you are going to live in Heaven? Depends on your choices today. Once and for all, decide to overcome the fear of death and love the life in God's eternity. This is possible when we honor the Creator of our life and live for others.

Do you know today what will happen after your death? I think it is easy enough to understand that we answer this question every day in our life, performing deeds and actions. With the help of the knowledge which we have gained from this book we should once and for all decide for ourselves where we will spend eternity.

Every day we have a choice whether to believe or not, whether to think about eternity or to hope that we will somehow receive Heaven. But the intent is clear: when we die we continue to exist somewhere. It might be an eternity in Hell, or in Heaven. Do not miss your chance to spend eternity in a beautiful place full of love. Someone decides to love people and to live life for others and others decide to be jealous and demand only from others, insisting that people make them happy. Someone decides to sacrifice his life, and resources for others and some decide to ignore those in need. This is the choice we should make today, how and where we will spend our eternity. Eternity is not a year, not in tens of years, time does not fit into the scope of eternity. So if you haven't decided yet what will happen after your death hurry to do it during your life because time is running out faster and we can't fix it.

While reading this book, together we painted a picture of the future. We have seen the benefits of Heaven, a place where life begins with colors and tastes and most important of all we have formed an interest of a real life in Heaven, where there are no restrictions, where everything breathes and lives only for love. By this, once and for all we

overcome the fear of death. With the help of this book, we were able to enjoy the benefits of death and see our future after the end of our life on Earth.

I invite each of you to delight in making Heaven, our final destination. A place where we will truly live in. Everyone has their own time and deadlines, but the one who does not live today as if it is the last day of his life has no opportunity to understand the value of the days he lived. Let's live today in freedom, without the fear of the future, in order to become rightful successors of Heaven which God has prepared for his children.

In order to be reconciled with God, one does not need to wait for death or a special occasion. Remember, you only have today to decide once and for all about your future in eternity after your death. Close your eyes to see Jesus Christ who is waiting with all his love just for you and will take you into the kingdom of eternal life. Say a confession prayer with simplicity and sincerity in the heart in order to free your life from fears, disbeliefs, and accept God as a Father into your life.

PRAYER OF CONFESSION

Dear Heavenly Father!
I come to you in prayer,
And, realize my sinfulness.
I believe in Your Word.
I believe that you accept all who come to you.
Dear Lord, forgive all my sins, have mercy upon me.
I do not want to live the same life. I want to belong to
you, Jesus!
Come into my heart, cleanse me. Be my Savior and
Shepherd. Guide my life.
I confess you, Jesus Christ, as my Lord.
I thank you that You hear my prayer, and by faith, I
accept Your salvation.
Thank You, my Savior.
Amen.

Bibliography

1. Scott Elwood "Paradise, the Holy City and the Glory of the Throne".

2. «The majority of Ukrainian families are childless» http://ru.tsn.ua/ukrayina/bolshinstvo-ukrainskih-semei-bezdetnye.html

3. "We build day after day for eternity". http://domnanebe.ru/index/nebes_svideteli/0-3

4. "Life after death is" http://goo.gl/aWk9N8

5. "Is death an illusion?" http://goo.gl/AO5xip

6. Kalinovsky P. " Last illness, death and after…".

7. "Scientists have proved the existence of the soul and even measure its weight". http://goo.gl/thB1oS

8. "Tommy Lee and Daisy Osborn - a life full of miracles". http://goo.gl/5khmwM

9. "Stories of survivors of clinical death". http://kliniksmert.ru/19-opisanie-raya.html

10. "Life after death". http://samaratoday.ru/news/151623

11.TMarkes G.G "I am leaving". http://goo.gl/doIeqC

12. "What is on the threshold of death?". http://goo.gl/EQZ5SO

13. "How were dying famous atheists". http://www.rusfront.ru/524-kak-umirali-znamenitye-ateisty.html

14. Mayer John "Voices From The Edge Of Eternity".

15. "If you find yourself in front of God what will you tell Him?".http://vk.com/video-37284517_163666280

16. "Atheist sciences start to believe in the existence of God". http://chtotakoe.org/news/science/2187/

17. "Science is increasingly convinced of the existence of God".http://inosmi.ru/world/20141227/225188475.html

18. "Life after death". http://goo.gl/kgxbQM

19. "Heaven is so close". http://kniga-java.wen.ru/nebesa.html

20. "How does Yuri die? The mysterious death of a hero of the space age". http://inosmi.ru/inrussia/20050728/221220.html

21. "Thinking out loud". http://www.lio.ru/archive/vera/75/03/vera_1975-03/magazine/article17.html

22. "Albert Einstein about God". http://spiritual-life. com.ua/ 2010/03/29/albert-ejnshtejn-o-boge/

23. "Stories of people that have experienced a clinical death". http://goo.gl/ciRu67

24. "The secret of Salvador Dali is not disclosed." http:// blogs.privet.ru/community/ilmondodellarte/58765914

25. "The story of Don Piper about clinical death". http://goo.gl/ZUsqkg

26. "Color mixing". http://www.kinkom.by/articles. php?id=12

27. "Going beyond the mind - it is a reality". http:// goo.gl/ufNEVI

28. Biryukov Y.V. "Life after death is, confirms scientist". http://www.mirvera.com/2013/04/blog-post_30. html

29. "A little bit of history". http://christianin.net.ru/ article.php?id=226

30. Ford Marvin "I went to Heaven". http://outpouring. ru/news/2009-03-18-514

SUNDAY ADELAJA'S
BIOGRAPHY

Pastor Sunday Adelaja is the Founder and Senior Pastor of The Embassy of the Blessed Kingdom of God for All Nations Church in Kyiv, Ukraine.

Sunday Adelaja is a Nigerian-born Leader, Thinker, Philosopher, Transformation Strategist, Pastor, Author and Innovator who lives in Kiev, Ukraine.

At 19, he won a scholarship to study in the former Soviet Union. He completed his master's program in Belorussia State University with distinction in journalism.

At 33, he had built the largest evangelical church in Europe — The Embassy of the Blessed Kingdom of God for All Nations.

Sunday Adelaja is one of the few individuals in our world who has been privileged to speak in the United Nations, Israeli Parliament, Japanese Parliament and the United States Senate.

The movement he pioneered has been instrumental in reshaping lives of people in the Ukraine, Russia and about 50 other nations where he has his branches.

His congregation, which consists of ninety-nine percent white Europeans, is a cross-cultural model of the church for the 21st century.

His life mission is to advance the Kingdom of God on earth by raising a generation of history makers who will live for a cause larger, bigger and greater than themselves. Those who will live like Jesus and transform every sphere of the society in every nation as a model of the Kingdom of God on earth.

His economic empowerment program has succeeded in raising over 200 millionaires in the short period of three years.

Sunday Adelaja is the author of over 300 books, many of which are translated into several languages including Russian, English, French, Chinese, German, etc.

His work has been widely reported by world media outlets such as The Washington Post, The Wall Street Journal, New York Times, Forbes, Associated Press, Reuters, CNN, BBC, German, Dutch and French national television stations.

Pastor Sunday is happily married to his "Princess" Bose Dere-Adelaja. They are blessed with three children: Perez, Zoe and Pearl.

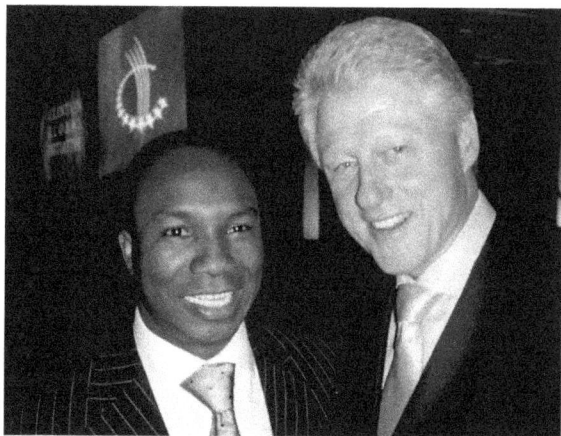

Bill Clinton —
42Nd President Of The
United States (1993–2001),
Former Arcansas State
Governor

Ariel "Arik" Sharon —
Israeli Politician, Israeli
Prime Minister (2001–2006)

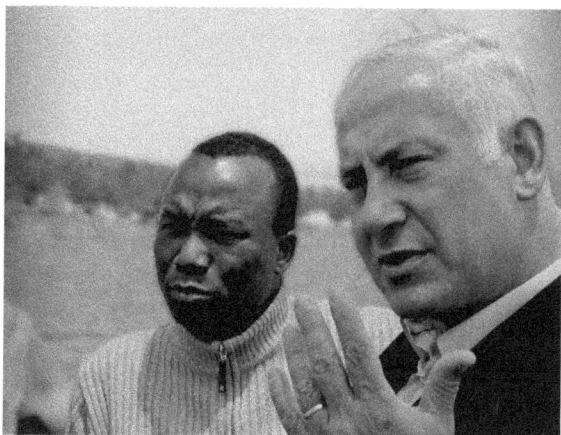

Benjamin Netanyahu —
Statesman Of Israel. Israeli
Prime Minister (1996–1999),
Acting Prime Minister
(From 2009)

Jean ChrEtien —
Canadian Politician,
20Th Prime Minister Of
Canada, Minister Of Justice
Of Canada, Head Of Liberan
Party Of Canada

Rudolph Giuliani —
American Political Actor,
Mayor Of New York Served
From 1994 To 2001. Actor
Of Republican Party

Colin Powell —
Is An American Statesman
And A Retired Four-Star
General In The Us Army,
65Th United States Secretary
Of State

Peter J. Daniels —
Is A Well-Known And
Respected Australian
Christian International
Business Statesman Of
Substance

Madeleine
Korbel Albright —
An American Politician And
Diplomat, 64[Th] United States
Secretary Of State

Kenneth Robert
Livingstone —
An English Politician,
1[St] Mayor Of London
(4 May 2000 – 4 May
2008), Labour Party
Representative

Sir Richard Charles Nicholas Branson —
English Business Magnate, Investor And Philanthropist. He Founded The *Virgin Group*, Which Controls More Than 400 Companies

Mel Gibson —
American Actor And Filmmaker

Chuck Norris —
American Martial Artist, Actor, Film Producer And Screenwriter

Christopher Tucker — American Actor And Comedian

Bernice Albertine King — American Minister Best Known As The Youngest Child Of Civil Rights Leaders Martin Luther King Jr. And Coretta Scott King Andrew

Andrew Young — American Politician, Diplomat, And Activist, 14[Th] United States Ambassador To The United Nations, 55[Th] Mayor Of Atlanta

General Wesley
Kanne Clark —
4-Star General And Nato
Supreme Allied Commander

Dr. Sunday Adelaja's family:
Perez, Pearl, Zoe and Pastor Bose Adelaja

FOLLOW
SUNDAY ADELAJA
ON SOCIAL MEDIA

Subscribe And Read Pastor Sunday's Blog:
www.sundayadelajablog.com

**Follow these links and listen to over 200
of Pastor Sunday`s Messages free of charge:**
http://sundayadelajablog.com/content/

Follow Pastor Sunday on Twitter:
www.twitter.com/official_pastor

**Join Pastor Sunday's Facebook
page to stay in touch:**
www.facebook.com/
pastor.sunday.adelaja

**Visit our websites for more
information about Pastor
Sunday's ministry:**
http://www.godembassy.com
http://www.
pastorsunday.com
http://sundayadelaja.de

CONTACT

BEST SELLING BOOKS BY DR. SUNDAY ADELAJA
AVAILABLE ON AMAZON.COM AND OKADABOOKS.COM

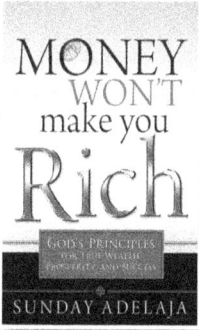

MONEY WON'T make you Rich — GOD'S PRINCIPLES FOR TRUE WEALTH, PROSPERITY AND SUCCESS — SUNDAY ADELAJA

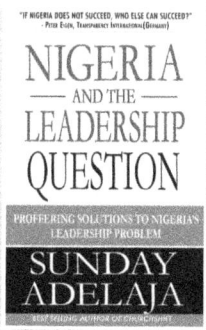

"IF NIGERIA DOES NOT SUCCEED, WHO ELSE CAN SUCCEED?" - PETER EIGEN, TRANSPARENCY INTERNATIONAL (GERMANY)

NIGERIA AND THE LEADERSHIP QUESTION — PROFFERING SOLUTIONS TO NIGERIA'S LEADERSHIP PROBLEM — SUNDAY ADELAJA — BEST SELLING AUTHOR OF CHURCHSHIFT

MYLES MUNROE — ... FINDING ANSWERS TO WHY GOOD PEOPLE DIE TRAGIC AND EARLY DEATHS — SUNDAY ADELAJA

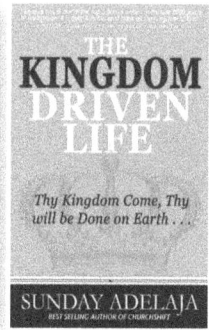

THE KINGDOM DRIVEN LIFE — Thy Kingdom Come, Thy will be Done on Earth . . . — SUNDAY ADELAJA — BEST SELLING AUTHOR OF CHURCHSHIFT

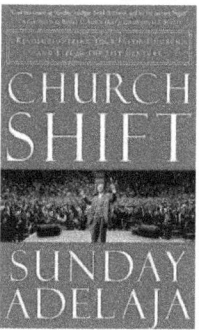

CHURCH SHIFT — SUNDAY ADELAJA

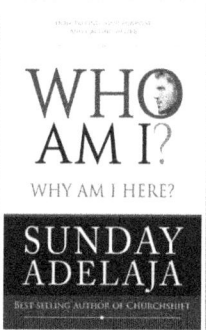

WHO AM I? WHY AM I HERE? — SUNDAY ADELAJA — BEST SELLING AUTHOR OF CHURCHSHIFT

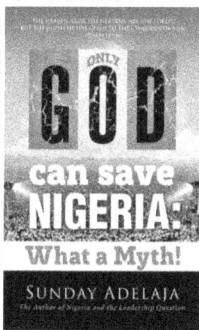

ONLY GOD can save NIGERIA: What a Myth! — SUNDAY ADELAJA — The Author of Nigeria and the Leadership Question

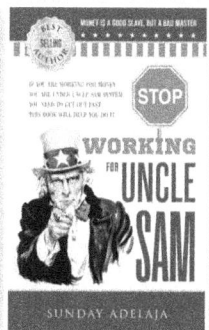

MONEY IS A GOOD SLAVE, BUT A BAD MASTER — STOP WORKING FOR UNCLE SAM — SUNDAY ADELAJA

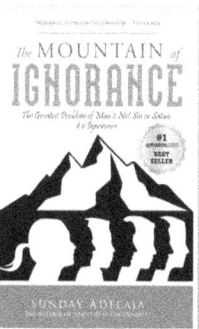

The MOUNTAIN of IGNORANCE — The Greatest Problem of Man is Not Sin or Satan, it is Ignorance — SUNDAY ADELAJA

OLORUNWA

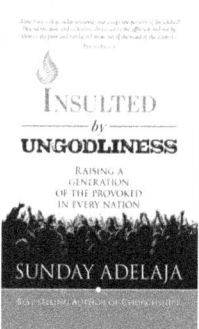

INSULTED by UNGODLINESS — RAISING A GENERATION OF THE PROVOKED IN EVERY NATION — SUNDAY ADELAJA — BEST SELLING AUTHOR OF CHURCHSHIFT

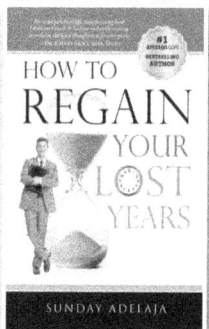

HOW TO REGAIN YOUR LOST YEARS — SUNDAY ADELAJA

BEST SELLING BOOKS BY DR. SUNDAY ADELAJA
AVAILABLE ON AMAZON.COM AND OKADABOOKS.COM

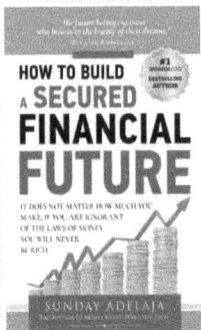

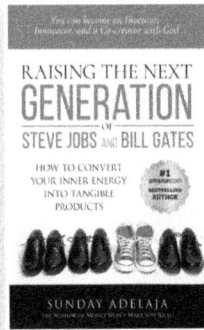

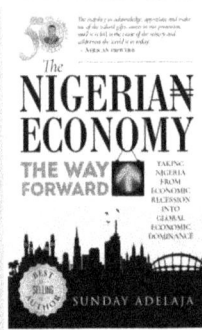

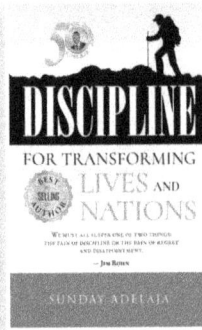

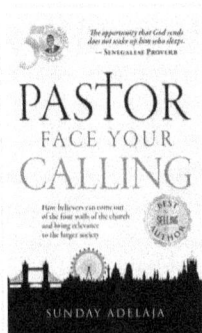

GOLDEN JUBILEE SERIES BOOKS
BY DR. SUNDAY ADELAJA

FOR DISTRIBUTION OR TO ORDER BULK COPIES OF THIS BOOKS, PLEASE CONTACT US:

USA | CORNERSTONE PUBLISHING
E-mail: info@thecornerstonepublishers.com, +1 (516) 547-4999
www.thecornerstonepublishers.com

AFRICA | SUNDAY ADELAJA MEDIA LTD.
E-mail: btawolana@hotmail.com
+2348187518530, +2348097721451, +2348034093699

LONDON, UK | PASTOR ABRAHAM GREAT
E-mail: abrahamagreat@gmail.com, +447711399828, +441908538141

KIEV, UKRAINE |
E-mail: pa@godembassy.org, Mobile: +380674401958

www.ingramcontent.com/pod-product-compliance
Lightning Source LLC
Chambersburg PA
CBHW022113080426

42734CB00006B/113